A Dream about this Book

About 5 years ago I had a very short dream I would like to share with you. In the dream I was looking at a book that I would write in the future. The book fell open to the middle because of inserts that had been placed there. These inserts reminded me of the free samples located in the middle of some women's magazines for perfumes and other products.

The inserts in my book were actually free samples of dress shirts in beautiful bright colors such as: pink, lavender, chartreuse, teal, and coral. They were starched and folded and the reader was able to take any one or all of them, if they desired. I was amazed that something so valuable would be included with the purchase of a book. I then woke up.

I asked other people to help me get an understanding of the dream, but never felt at peace about any of their interpretations. God revealed the dream's meaning only a few months before this book went to print. **You are holding the book from that dream in your hands**.

God's interpretation: the shirts represent the varied, amazingly beautiful, and gifted personalities of the people who will read this book. This book will offer them, maybe for the first time, the freedom to choose to be themselves apart from any influence which may have pressured them to be someone they are not. The shirts were all brightly colored because every personality is one-of-a-kind, uniquely crafted by God. Therefore, each one boldly stands out in their own uniqueness. The freedom to take or leave the shirts was left up to the reader with no pressure whatsoever. This represents God's gracious offer of freedom without any obligation. The shirts could even be taken out later since they were nicely folded and did not interfere with the reading of the book. This represents God's timing for some who will not be able to embrace their total freedom right away, but will come back to select it later.

My motivation for writing has been the joy of knowing the freedom you will experience by realizing you are completely loved and uniquely created by God. While reading this book, you may remember desires of your heart long forgotten. This is the Spirit of God setting you free to be yourself. Don't be afraid to pick your brightly colored shirt and wear it for all the world to see. According to the dream, in God's mind, there are no dull colors (personalities). You are a one-of-a-kind creation, and I pray you will embrace that fact as much as God does. *"You are the light of the world. A city that is set on a hill cannot be hidden. Nor do they light a lamp and put it under a basket, but on a lampstand, and it gives light to all who are in the house. Let your light so shine before men, that they may see your good works and glorify your Father in heaven"* (Matthew 5:14-16).

Satan's overwhelming goal has been to put your light out, but he has failed. You are still here and you are still pursuing God. The church is about to arise to her finest hour when she will embrace the uniqueness of the individual believer with the same passion she will embrace her oneness in Christ. *"... A people come, great and strong. The like of whom has never been; nor will there ever be any such after them, even for many successive generations... Every one marches in formation, and they do not break ranks. They do not push one another; every one marches in his own column. Though they lunge between the weapons, they are not cut down....The earth quakes before them, the heavens tremble; the sun and the moon grow dark, and the stars diminish their brightness. The Lord gives voice before His army, for His camp is very great; for strong is the One who executes His word"* (Joel 2:2,7b,8,10,11a).

The Battle for Your Heart

How to Fight Back

The Battle for Your Heart

ISBN: 978-0-692-25475-2
Library of Congress Control Number: 2014914241
Copyright © 2014

Published by Michael Braun

Prepared for publishing by:
Orion Productions, LLC.
PO Box 51194
Colorado Springs, CO 80949
www.orion316.tv

Editor: Cande Maxie

Dedication

I would like to dedicate this book to a particular group of my brothers and sisters in Christ. You are the ones who have never really been understood. You were willing to ask questions that no one else would, and deal with problems that no one else apparently seemed to have. You may have even been "encouraged" to pull yourself together, or just been tolerated. But you knew in your heart something was just not right. Even though some of you felt as though you had, to your credit, you did not give up.

This book is dedicated to your passion. God is well pleased with you. It has been an honor to write for you, knowing God's desire is to answer the passionate cry of your heart. I hope this book is a confirmation to your spirit of what God has been trying to convey all along. You are His champions. May this work be the weapon you needed to defend His honor.

Acknowledgements

I would like to thank most of all my friend and editor Cande Maxie. Without her heart for this project, the finished product would look nothing like it does today. If this book touches you without offending, she is the one responsible for making that happen. Cande, you have renewed my faith in what the church can do if she is in agreement and I thank you from the bottom of my heart. Know that all who read this will benefit from the gifts God has placed in you.

I would also like to thank the students and faculty of Charis Bible College in Washington D.C. Your hunger for the truth of this message was strong enough to inspire me through the difficulties of getting this material in print. Know that all who read this will benefit from your passion for God.

Table of Contents

Section 4 Resist, Don't Assist, Your Enemy

Introduction

This is a book about dreaming; a book about becoming child-like again; a book about imagining with God and being able to believe that, even though God's plan seems too good to be true it is even better than that. This is a book about discovering who you are and who you are really meant to be. To get to this place of freedom you must fight your way through a continuous barrage of lies. There is only one way to your place of victory: through the opposition of your enemy.

What if I told you that the assault on truth was a strategically planned attack? That it was systematic, unending, and launched purposefully in the mind of every single individual to keep you from ever meeting the Truth. The Truth is a person: Jesus. *"I am the way, and the truth, and the life..."* (John 14:6a). This book is about truth, but it may seem to be more about lies because there is only one Truth (Jesus) and many lies.

The goal of this book is that by seeing clearly the lies of Satan, your enemy, you will be able to walk in the counsel of God's truth, and thereby avoid the influence of lies in your life. I can tell you, without reservation, that God is eager to set you free from all deceptions. It says in Galatians 5:1, *"It was for freedom that Christ set us free..."* (NASB). You see, God and His Son are both Deliverers. The heart of a deliverer is not to incrementally dole out freedom, but to set the captives free. The process of apprehending your freedom will take a giant step forward as you begin to see more clearly the influence of deception in your life.

Blessed be the Lord my Rock,
Who trains my hands for war,
And my fingers for battle —
My lovingkindness and my fortress,
My high tower and my deliverer,
My shield and the One in whom I take refuge,
Who subdues my people under me (Psalms 144:1-2).

Section 1

Knowing Who You Were Made To Be

The things you don't understand
cost you a price that you never realize you paid.

Chapter 1

Why Were You Created?

Is God relational?

I would like to begin by destroying one of the most powerful lies that has ever existed: God is distant and not interested in relating to you. How could that lie be even remotely possible? <u>God's entire being is an ongoing relationship</u>! God exists as three separate beings who are really one: God the Father, God the Son, and God the Holy Spirit. They are known as the Trinity – individually separate, but uniquely One. Here is a very important question to unlock the reason you were created. What has always existed between the personalities within the Trinity? The answer is <u>relationship</u>. You may have never considered this fact, but relationship is one of the very few things which is eternal. God has always been in relationship.

God's desire is to live in relationship or there would not
be a Trinity.

You were created by a relational God to be in relationship with Him. God's desire is to live in relationship or there would not be a Trinity. Relationship is one of the attributes that makes God Who He is. Without relationship we are not discussing the one true God, but another god fabricated from lies we have believed. <u>Never again be deceived by the lie of a distant non-relational God</u>. God has an unlimited capacity for relationship, and His desire is to have a relationship with you personally. That is the ultimate reason you were created. However, in order to have a relationship there must be communication.

How does God talk with you?

The answer I am about to give for the above question may shock you. I don't know how God talks to you, for the same reason I am unaware of how your husband or wife kisses you. This is because your relationship with God is uniquely personal. <u>The misunderstood assumption of the above question is that God talks to everyone the same way</u>. This is not true. The way God communicates with you is a personal experience which will be different from the way He communicates with anyone else. For example, even if you try, you cannot have the exact same relationship with each of your children, and neither does God try to relate to each of His children the same way. This is because: <u>there is no formula for relationship</u>.

The knowledge that God wants to have a distinct relationship with you exposes another common lie (stronghold) embraced by many believers. The lie is: you cannot hear from God. I may not know the specifics of how God talks to you personally, but I do know, no matter what lies you hear to the contrary, you can hear from God and recognize His voice. *"And when he brings out his own sheep, he*

*goes before them; and the sheep follow him, <u>for they know his voice</u>.
Yet they will by no means follow a stranger, but will flee from him, for
they do not know the voice of strangers" (John 10:4-5).* The thought
that you can't hear God, even if you are the one repeating it, is still
not true. The above passage is the truth.

God is broadcasting all the time. The question is: What is blocking your reception?

I will not be directly addressing how to hear from God in this
book, but I will be addressing the lies that are telling you that <u>you
can't</u>. I believe that once the lies are dealt with, you will begin to
hear the communication you previously were unable to receive. God
is broadcasting all the time. The question is: What is blocking your
reception? Throughout this book I will be referencing God speaking to
me in a variety of ways. However, I have the greatest respect for your
individual relationship with God, and I know His communication
with you will be different than my own. Satan will attempt to trick
some of you into comparing how we both hear from God. Don't fall
into this comparison trap. We will be addressing that lie in Chapter
13. No one hears from God exactly the same way. If you do not have
a lot of stories to tell about hearing from God, you will.

Who receives God's affection?

You were created for a relationship; to be the bride for God's only
Son. You were created to be the recipient of God's affection. You were
created to be the one the Son of God can lavish His love upon for all
eternity. <u>The extent to which you can believe this foundational truth is
the extent to which you can be free in every way</u>. All the lies addressed
in this book lose their power once you comprehend your value in the

eyes of Jesus, our Groom and future Husband. You may have never heard this before, but I will show you it is true and explain its application to your life. I believe, as you read further, your destiny will unfold as you embrace the knowledge of how much God loves you.

As your children grow older you, as a good parent, desire for them to meet a special someone, marry, and spend the rest of their lives together. You hope this would be someone with whom they can share their heart's dreams and desires. This deepest of all relationships, the marriage relationship, was instituted by God to provide an outlet of sacrificial giving which would teach true love; the very heart of God. As parents, we acquired this desire for our children from God, our spiritual Father. If we desire an exceptional soul mate for our children, and that desire originated from God, then how did God deal with that desire for His son, Jesus? God had no one available in eternity to be that extraordinary someone for His only Son. For God, the solution was simple; He created a wife!

Have you ever heard this quoted, "If a tree falls in the woods and no one is there, does it make a sound?" The real question being asked is, does it make any difference without someone to hear? God knows how great His Son is, but who receives the benefit if no one is there to receive His love? God's Son is not just a nice guy; He is Love Himself. But, outside of the Trinity, who will know? God's desire is for there to be someone who can fully experience the greatness of His Son in the deepest possible way. You were created to be that special someone, His bride. Sadly, most people are hindered from drawing close enough to God to hear the sound of His love.

This is a peculiar analogy, but nevertheless true: You can only kiss one person at a time. God's affection is the same way. Each relationship He has is personal; it is not a group relationship. God is not loving on the mass of humanity in one big kiss. He has many relationships, yet they are all one-on-one. He relates to one man or one woman at a time. His relationship with you is exclusive; a unique relationship that He experiences with no one else. You are truly one of a kind, and your Creator is the One Who knows exactly why He made you the way He did.

Do I have a choice?

The first line on the left in **Diagram A** on the following page says, "Creation of the Future Wife." Notice that it says future wife. In a society of free will, which is how God's kingdom functions, no one is coerced into marrying. This is by no means an arranged marriage. You are perfectly capable of rejecting the Son of God's proposal of marriage; but know, when you reject His offer, you are rejecting your purpose for existing in the first place. You are literally rejecting the relationship that determines your destiny. We accept God's offer of a life spent with Him the same way that any bride does by being selected, being asked, and saying, "Yes". In John 15:16 Jesus says, *"You did not choose Me, but I chose you and appointed you that you should go and bear fruit"*.

As we look at a story from the Old Testament in Genesis 24, we can see this freedom to accept or reject the offer of marriage clearly illustrated. Abraham had sent his servant to find a wife for his son, Isaac, from his own lineage. The servant was miraculously led to one young lady, Rebekah, who was Abraham's relative. She was supernaturally selected by God through a sign. But, even after this miraculous event had occurred, we read in verse 58 of chapter 24, *"Then they called Rebekah and said to her, 'Will you go with this man?' And she said, 'I will go.'"* Rebekah still had the right of refusal no matter how supernatural the arrangement had been. In the same

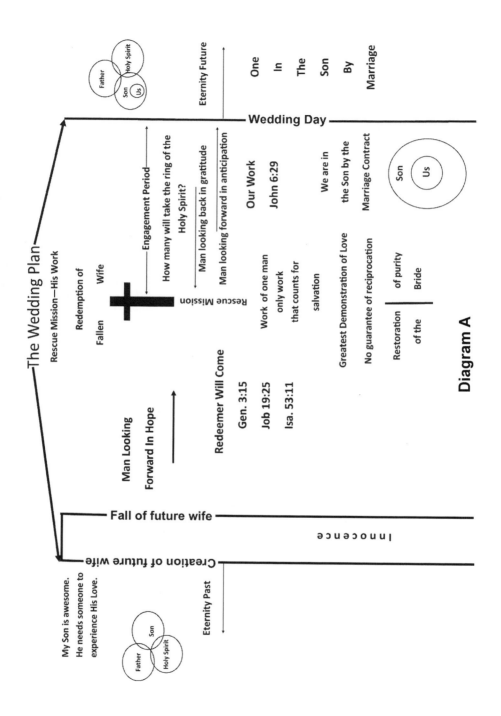

The Wedding Plan

Rescue Mission—His Work

My Son is awesome. He needs someone to experience His Love.

Eternity Past

Creation of future wife

Innocence

Fall of future wife

Man Looking Forward In Hope

Redeemer Will Come

Gen. 3:15
Job 19:25
Isa. 53:11

Redemption of

Fallen   Wife

Rescue Mission

Engagement Period

How many will take the ring of the Holy Spirit?

Man looking back in gratitude
Man looking forward in anticipation

Wedding Day

Eternity Future

One
In
The
Son
By
Marriage

Our Work

John 6:29

We are in the Son by the Marriage Contract

Son / Us

Work of one man only work that counts for salvation

Greatest Demonstration of Love

No guarantee of reciprocation

Restoration of purity of the Bride

Father / Holy Spirit / Son / Us

Father / Son / Holy Spirit

Diagram A

manner God has supernaturally arranged your destiny to be the wife of His only Son, but you still have the free will to reject the proposal.

One of the hardest things to do in this cruel fallen world we live in, is to accept the fact that we are loved as much as we truly are.

You have most likely never heard that you were created to be the object of affection for Jesus Christ, God's Son. One of the hardest things to do in this cruel, fallen world we live in, is to accept the fact that we are loved as much as we truly are. It seems surreal against the backdrop of all the hatred and violence we see every day on the news. There may be many of you who have accepted God's proposal, but still question your worth. My objective is for you to be delivered from these doubts. I pray, as you read on, you will completely accept your worth and, through that knowledge, embrace your destiny.

How good was it in the beginning?

After Adam and Eve were created the world was a joyful place. God was happy for His Son because of the gift He had created for Him. The Son was excited about His new relationship with mankind and the Holy Spirit rejoiced to see the love they both shared for the Father's new creation, His bride. This was a time of relational purity in which they communicated directly with God face to face. Adam and Eve continued in this state of innocence for an undetermined length of time. Their innocence was so complete that, even though naked, they communicated with God totally unashamed. They were utterly naïve, carefree, and innocent just like little children.

This remarkable time of peace and contentment was abruptly ended when they lost their innocence. I have labeled this: Fall of Future Wife (**Diagram A**). I sometimes will interchange the terms

<u>bride</u> and <u>wife</u>, because of God's mindset toward marriage. His mindset toward marriage was instilled in the Hebrew culture and there are many Bible stories paralleling how God relates to us, His bride. Here is a perfect example.

In the historical account of Jesus birth in Mathew 1:19-20, Joseph, Jesus's earthly father, discovered that Mary was pregnant and he was going to put her away secretly. This meant that he was going to divorce Mary, his fiancé, because she was pregnant. An angel told Joseph, in a dream, that Mary had not been unfaithful and the Child was the Son of God. Therefore, Joseph did not go through with the divorce. In Hebrew culture, the engagement contract was so binding that the couple was considered married once the contract was signed, even though the marriage had not been physically consummated. In order to terminate the engagement, Joseph was obligated to divorce his fiancé. One spiritual parallel is that our contract as the bride of Christ is not easily broken. We are already united with God through the acceptance of the bride price paid for us: the life of Jesus. We are regarded as contractually married to God in Christ. The parallel of this spiritually is that once you have said yes to Jesus, in God's mind, the union is complete. When you accept Christ, as far as God is concerned, you are His. Ephesians 1:14 even calls us, *"the purchased possession"*.

Who is the bride of Christ?

The church is not a building and it is not an institution. The church is the bride of Christ. God sees the church as the relationships between Jesus and the unique individuals who make up His bride. The Greek word for church used in the New Testament is <u>Ecclesia</u> which means: a calling out. But, what does this definition have to do with being a bride?

Now, let me ask a simple question that will explain perfectly how the definition "called out ones" relates to being the bride. Once you put an engagement ring on your finger what are you called out from? When I am speaking to a group of people, usually a young lady will yell out the obvious answer: "Every other man"! When a proposal has been accepted it is understood that both parties have been called out from all other close personal relationships with the opposite sex. When we relate this to our acceptance of God's proposal it means that we are His alone and are called out from all others, hence the name Ecclesia for God's bride, His church. The church has been called out from the world. *"If you were of the world, the world would love its own. Yet because you are not of the world, but I chose you out of the world, therefore the world hates you" (John 15:19).* Although we are in the world we are not part of the world. Since we are in God's church we have a different covenant relationship with Him than those who have not accepted His offer. We are exclusively God's.

Once you have said yes to God, it is important to understand the exclusivity of your commitment. In our modern culture there is a perspective among some Christians that we can do what we please, as long as we have accepted God's offer. But, how would you feel if you saw someone who was engaged to be married involved in many intimate relationships? All of us would immediately consider this as inappropriate because the very nature of saying yes to marrying one person inherently means, you said no to everyone else.

Failing to be aware of the need to separate ourselves from the lusts and passions that could control our heart, is evidence that we have not understood the meaning of our exclusive relationship with God. This separation from other attachments cannot be accomplished by our own efforts, but only by experiencing how much God loves us. In most engagements, it is not at all difficult for the couple to forget about everyone else because they are completely immersed in their love for each other. The separation from other attachments is completely natural if authentic love is present.

How big is the gospel?

Jesus' work on the cross was a premeditated and very well executed rescue mission.

What I am about to say may sound as if I am downplaying Jesus's bearing of our sins on the cross. Usually when someone refers to the gospel, the good news, they mean that Jesus came and died on the cross to take our place so that we would not be punished forever for our sins. This is very good news, indeed! However, in relation to the story of mankind's reason for being created, it is only part of a much grander story. I think it will help all of us if we can see the bigger picture. I often refer to Jesus's work on the cross as the rescue. The overall reason we were created is the full extent of the gospel: to be the bride of Christ. Jesus's work on the cross was a premeditated and very well executed rescue mission to restore His bride back to her intended place. I will explain in detail that the bigger picture of the gospel is more than the rescue itself; it is more awe inspiring than most of us realize.

The reason Jesus came to earth was bigger than saving you from the consequences of your sin. The reason Jesus came to earth was to rescue you so that you could fulfill your purpose. Jesus came to earth to save a wedding. The cross is the strategy He used to achieve that outcome. In the New Testament in 1 John 3:8 it says, *"...For this reason the Son of God was manifest, that He might destroy the works of the devil."* What works of the devil is the passage referring to? Since Jesus came to earth to solve the problem, then it must be referring to Satan's work carried out on earth. His work was executed in the Garden of Eden through deception. It was this deception which caused mankind to sin and be separated from God. The reason Jesus came to earth in human form was to destroy the results of this evil work: deception.

What is the foundation of deception?

Deception is built on the foundation of lies, but lies are a new phenomenon. In the grand scheme of all eternity, lies have not existed very long. One of the first deceptions which ever took place was in the Garden of Eden when Satan, in the form of a serpent, deceived man using the insinuated lie: God is withholding something from you. Before this documented deception, there had only been truth for all of eternity. The significance of this is staggering.

The standard for all of eternity is truth. Lies originated much later only for the purpose of opposing that eternal standard.

Truth is the standard we were created to live under. In our hearts we desire what we were made for: truth not deception. This explains why, as humans, we are predisposed to desire the truth and are not equally receptive to lies. The standard for all of eternity is truth. Lies originated much later only for the purpose of opposing this eternal standard. Good and evil are not equal and have not co-existed for eternity. God has existed eternally as good and one of His created beings, Satan (originally named Lucifer), rebelled. Evil originated at the time of his rebellion and soon after, Satan originated lies. John 8:44 says, *"You are of your father the devil, and the desires of your* *father you want to do. He was a murderer from the beginning, and does not stand in the truth, because there is no truth in him. When he speaks a lie, he speaks from his own resources, <u>for he is a liar and the father of it</u>."* Who will rescue us from our deceptions? Jesus Christ – The Truth (John 14:6).

Chapter 2

Why Is Jesus the Wedding Savior?

Who is God passionate about?

Since mankind was created to be the bride of Christ, when man sinned they were unfaithful to the Groom. God is still passionately in love with mankind because His love never changes so, here is the obstacle that must be overcome. How is the Holy Son of God supposed to marry someone who is no longer innocent? We now have an unfaithful bride who was created with the intended purpose of marrying a Holy God, and now there is no way this is possible! Because God cannot be reduced to the level of fallen man, there is only one solution. Man must be brought up to the level of God's holiness. There is but one way for the union to go forward; God Himself must restore His bride's purity. He alone has the passionate love and holy capability to succeed in such a rescue.

Jesus makes His impure bride pure again at the cross by using His own blood to make the marriage covenant legal.

Jesus is going to come and purchase back His bride's purity with His own holy blood. When a women has not been with a man before marriage, there is blood when the marriage is consummated. At the moment mankind sinned, they defiled themselves with the devil. There is no longer innocent blood to seal the covenant of marriage. In order to make the marriage covenant legal Jesus, at the cross, makes His impure bride pure again by using His own sinless blood. At the cross, Jesus makes His impure bride pure again by using His own sinless blood thereby making the marriage covenant legal.

No matter what horrible sins you have committed in your life, when you accept Jesus's offer, your sins are washed away and you are as pure as snow. In our minds the earthly memories may linger, but as far as God is concerned, it is as if they never happened. If you are thinking that this could not be possible, then remember this whole mission was humanly impossible, yet God did it! Psalms 103:11-12 says it this way, *"For as the heavens are high above the earth, so great is His mercy toward those who fear Him; as far as the east is from the west, so far has he removed our transgressions from us."* The distance between east and west cannot be measured. Yet, that is how far you can be separated from your sin by believing in the work that Jesus did for you, His bride.

You are the joy set before Christ.

Jesus Christ is "The Wedding Savior". He came to buy His bride out of sin and save His Own wedding. *"Looking unto Jesus, the author and finisher of our faith, who for the joy that was set before*

Him endured the cross, despising the shame, and has sat down at the right hand of the throne of God" (Hebrews 12:2). When I teach, I often ask the audience if they know what the joy set before Christ is. The highest percentage of the audience that has known the answer was about five percent. I cannot fully explain how that grieves the Holy Spirit. His mission is to reveal to you what has been given to you by God through the marriage covenant. *"Now we have received, not the spirit of the world, but the Spirit who is from God, that we might know the things that have been freely given to us by God" (1 Corinthians 2:12).*

You are the joy set before Christ! You are the reason He endured the cross. He despised your shame because it separated your relationship with Him. Therefore, He removed it by taking it upon Himself at the cross. After He finished His work, He sat down. I was feeling frustrated about people not realizing their worth to God and I wrote the following song. May the revelation of your importance burn like a fire in your heart as you understand, more deeply, the love God has for you.

You can tap it here or go to www.TheTruthWins.org/go/TheOne

The One You Love

I am the joy that was set before Christ;
I am the reason there is dance in His life.
I am the smile God sees on His face;
I am the reason He showed His grace.

I am the one you love.
I am the one you love.

He set His eyes upon a prize,
And that prize it was me.
Hallelujah this gospel has set me free.
Hallelujah this gospel has set me free.

I am the one you love.
I am the one you love.

The church will arise with fire in her eyes,
And then she will see
The flaming eyes of the One who is her's for eternity.
Hallelujah your love has captured me.
Hallelujah your love has captured me.

I am the one you love.
I am the one you love.
I am the one you love.

I am the joy that was set before Christ;
I am the reason there is dance in His life.
I am the smile God sees on His face;
I am the reason He showed His grace.

I am the one you love.
I am the one you love.
I am the one you love.

Why is there a conflict in Cana?

To better understand the bigger picture of the gospel it will be helpful to look at the biblical account of Jesus's first miracle recorded in John 2:1-11.

"On the third day there was a wedding in Cana of Galilee, and the mother of Jesus was there. Now both Jesus and His disciples were invited to the wedding. And when they ran out of wine, the mother of Jesus said to Him, "They have no wine." Jesus said to her, "Woman, what does your concern have to do with Me? My hour has not yet come." His mother said to the servants, "Whatever He says to you, do it." Now there were set there six waterpots of stone, according to the manner of purification of the Jews, containing twenty or thirty gallons apiece. Jesus said to them, "Fill the waterpots with water." And they filled them up to the brim. And He said to them, "Draw some out now, and take it to the master of the feast." And they took it. When the master of the feast had tasted the water that was made wine, and did not know where it came from (but the servants who had drawn the water knew), the master of the feast called the bridegroom. And he said to him, "Every man at the beginning sets out the good wine, and when the guests have well drunk, then the inferior. You have kept the good wine until now!" This beginning of signs Jesus did in Cana of Galilee, and manifested His glory; and His disciples believed in Him."

Taking into consideration the animosity that already existed between Jesus and Satan, I believe there is a lot more going on at the wedding in Cana than appears on the surface. When two fighters enter a ring, both walk to the middle and have what is called a "stare down." They look into each other's eyes for signs of fear and try to intimidate their opponent. I believe the situation at this wedding is similar. Satan knows Jesus and His disciples are in attendance. He sees this as an opportunity to bring shame on the groom's family by exploiting their financial situation. Satan also has the added bonus of flaunting his authority over mankind in the face of Jesus. Is Satan saying, "This is my ring (earth) and I am the strongest one here?"

Running out of wine would be an indication that the groom may be unable to provide adequately for his new wife. The shame of this would be horrific. The bride's father would also have reservations about giving his consent to the marriage contract, supposing he may have chosen the wrong man for his daughter. This will be a disgrace on the family. Shame is Satan's main weapon at this wedding. The scenario has been set and, if Satan achieves his goal, the trust and intimacy of this couple will be ruined on their first day together.

Shame was also Satan's main weapon to reinforce mankind's guilt in the Garden of Eden. Shame is what drove man to hide from God after their sin rather than approach Him for forgiveness. Without agreeing with the shame, man could have come to God repentant and vulnerable. The separation we see in the garden was not God's choice. The separation was not because God could not be near a sinner, as most of us have been taught. God had a relationship with Cain even after he murdered his brother, Abel. Jesus was openly accused of eating with tax collectors and sinners. The separation was not from God's side of the relationship, but man's. Satan is an expert at destroying relationships, and shame is one of the main tools he uses to achieve that end. At this wedding, Satan is doing what he does best: killing, stealing and destroying. But, this event is unique because Jesus is present. In my opinion, Satan is testing the strength of Jesus, his opponent.

Whose shame does Jesus despise?

Most of my life I have held an incorrect understanding of the concept of shame mentioned in Hebrews 12:2: *"...who for the joy that was set before Him, endured the cross, <u>despising the shame</u>, and has sat down at the right hand of the throne of God."* I had always believed that, while on the cross, Jesus was despising His own shame of being naked and being made a public spectacle. This interpretation is incorrect. The Greek word used for <u>shame</u> in Hebrews 12:2 means: dishonesty or disgrace. In Hebrews 6:6 the same writer spoke of shame, but used a different word when he referenced Jesus's crucifixion: *"if they fall away, to renew them again to repentance, since they crucify again for themselves the Son of God, and <u>put Him to an open shame</u>."* The Greek word for <u>shame</u> used here means: to make a public example. If the shame referred to in Hebrews 12:2 had been Jesus's public humiliation the writer would have used this same word. He was inspired to use a different word.

Jesus is incapable of having shame of His own because he has never done anything to be ashamed of.

The shame that Jesus despised was the shame caused by mankind's guilt over their sin. Jesus despised our shame, so He chose to take it away. He took the penalty for our sins, and by removing the sin He removed the shame. Jesus is incapable of having shame of His own because he has never done anything to be ashamed of. He did experience our shame by receiving it into His own body on the cross; *"who Himself bore our sins in His own body on the tree, that we, having died to sins, might live for righteousness - by whose stripes you were healed" (1 Peter 2:24).* God knows the shame we feel, and He despises the way Satan brings shame by manipulating our feelings of guilt. A war has been fought and won to give you the right to walk shamelessly in the freedom provided by your Liberator, Jesus Christ. At this wedding Jesus is demonstrating that He will remove man's need to wash away shame. He will replace man's shame with the in-filling of the Holy Spirit, which is represented by the wine

Why is Satan frustrated with Jesus?

I believe Satan is beginning to get frustrated trying to understand this God in-the-flesh battle plan. At this point Satan has been waiting for over 30 years without a clear understanding of Jesus's mission. Remember, Jesus had done nothing miraculous before this impending miracle in Cana. A short while before this wedding, Satan had tempted Jesus in the wilderness. His temptations, which had been successful on other men, had no effect on Jesus. Jesus is unlike any man Satan has ever encountered. Satan had known Jesus as Deity, also as the commander of the armies of Heaven, but I believe this God/man strategy is way over Satan's head. *"Which none of the rulers of this age knew; for had they known, they would not have crucified the Lord of glory" (1 Corinthians 2:8).*

Is Satan taunting Jesus at this wedding with his lawful control over man? Is he saying, "I have dominion over mankind and I can do whatever I want to"? Is he saying, "What are you going to do about it"? Is this a form of retaliation for His recent loss in the wilderness? I am not completely sure, but when I explain the ramifications of what Jesus did by turning the water to wine, it feels like round 2.

Why does God value motive over method?

I want to make a point about the emphasis that has always been placed on the act of turning water to wine. In fact, in my Bible written above this story is the title, "Water Turned to Wine." Part of Satan's deception has been to distort the emphasis of this miracle. God is not a God of methods; He is a God of motives. It is not how you do something, but why you do it that matters with God. Jesus was not trying to show He could convert molecules of H2O into molecules of wine. Jesus can do anything He wants with water. He made it! He can walk on it; He can push it up into walls and have people walk on dry land through the middle of it; He can even make mud with it and heal people. He is not doing this to display His ability as a Miracle Worker, but to deliver this couple He loves from shame.

David did not kill the lion, the bear, or Goliath with the same weapon. But, he killed them all with a heart motivated by protection for his sheep and strong confidence in His covenant with God. He possibly used a sling to kill Goliath because he was too tall for David to hit him in the head with a club. The point is, God cares about the heart. It is never good to get caught up in methods. Jesus healed in a wide variety of ways, but each time it was from a heart of love for those He was healing. It is important that we stay focused on the motives and not the methods. Jesus's motive for turning water to wine was out of His love. He loved the couple and He hated the shame they would experience. Jesus is "The Wedding Savior", not a winemaker.

Why is the Cana wedding not a coincidence?

The first thing that Jesus is asked to do in His earthly ministry is to save a wedding. One of the first things He will do when we all arrive in Heaven is be the Groom at our wedding. I do not believe this is a coincidence. At this wedding in Cana, Jesus is taking another look at the heart commitment He made long ago in Heaven. A wedding is the beginning of a long commitment and here Jesus is renewing His commitment to our rescue. For Jesus to see what was about to take place at this wedding, without His intervention, is a reminder to Him of His purpose for coming to earth. This is not about turning water to wine; this is about Jesus removing the shame from His bride.

Jesus will destroy the devil's scheme by taking the water that was used for ceremonial washing and rendering it unusable. This was the water that was used by men so they could say they had made themselves clean before God. He will turn this water, which could only be used for man's outward physical cleansing, into wine which represents the Holy Spirit of God. As wine is taken internally and changes the heart of the drinker, people can only be truly changed by the Holy Spirit coming into their hearts. Outward cleansing will never be enough to produce a new birth. It is only through an intimate relationship with the Holy Spirit, Who is taken into our heart, that something completely new can be birthed. *"Therefore, if anyone is in Christ, he is a new creation; old things have passed away; behold, all things have become new" (2 Corinthians 5:17)*. No one is in Christ unless they have taken His Spirit into their heart.

Why does God hate self-righteousness?

At the same time Jesus saves the wedding, He stops man's self-righteous washing.

God hates man's attempts at self-righteousness because they interfere with His Own acceptable restoration of our relationship with Him. *"Then the Lord said to him, 'Now you Pharisees make* the outside of the cup and dish clean, but your inward part is full of greed and wickedness'" (Luke 11:39). Man's attempt at righteousness can never go deep enough to solve the sin problem. At the same time Jesus saves the wedding, He stops man's self-righteous washing.

At the wedding they had been drinking a lot and that is why they are out of wine. There are plenty of empty wine skins available, so why doesn't Jesus just refill the old wine skins? He could have easily created the new wine in the old wine skins. This would have demonstrated His power and stopped the impending shame at this wedding just as effectively. Jesus purposely selected those ceremonial water pots used for man's attempted purification. He is making a very deliberate point at this wedding.

The first miracle Jesus performed on earth broke the power of self-righteous works. He used the changing of water to wine to display His hatred of self-righteousness. He demonstrated that His kingdom would be established by His Spirit **only** and not by the works of men done in their own power. No one who now comes to this wedding will be able to purify themselves. Likewise, no one coming to the wedding supper of the Lamb of God will be able to purify themselves. To experience the joy of the wedding, their only choice will be to drink of God's Spirit, represented by the wine.

All the work of God's Kingdom is accomplished by God Himself.

All the work of God is done by His Spirit Who is represented by the wine which must be taken into man for him to be changed. In Zechariah 4:6 God said, "Not by might nor by power, but by my Spirit, says the Lord of Host." All the work of God's kingdom is accomplished by God Himself. Jesus clearly reveals this at the wedding in Cana. No work of man, apart from the indwelling Holy Spirit, accomplishes anything in the Kingdom of God! For the indwelling of the Holy Spirit to take place, Jesus must first accomplish the rescue mission. Jesus, at this wedding, was demonstrating what would be accomplished by His rescue mission: the indwelling of God's Holy Spirit within His bride. Jesus shows that God, Himself, will come to live in man. Jesus openly reveals His mission for coming to earth to Satan, a self-absorbed fallen angel, who has no ability whatsoever to understand this selfless plan.

God makes it clear to all of us here in Cana that the work needed to save His bride is only possible from His side of the separation. Any delusions that we have of saving ourselves must be abandoned in order to receive the free gift of the Holy Spirit. We will never be able to restore the relationship by our own efforts. In order to make that perfectly clear, Jesus picked the ceremonial washing pots at this wedding. The foundation of the Gospel is that only God Himself, in Christ, can save the wedding. *"...that God was in Christ reconciling the world to Himself..." (2Cor. 5:19).*

The shame of our sin can compel us to perform self-righteous works rather than face the vulnerability needed for intimacy. Many of us can stay busy in religious activity as a cover-up to avoid the vulnerability of a relationship with God. This is nothing new. In fact, man's first reaction to the shame of sin was to start a sewing business. Genesis 3:7 says, *"Then the eyes of both of them were opened, and they knew that they were naked; and they sewed fig leaves together and made themselves coverings."* I have a very simple definition of <u>self-righteous works</u>: to cover one's self. There was always another option in the Garden of Eden for Adam and Eve. They could have come to God repentant, vulnerable, and naked. Shame and fear stopped that action, but it would have been the quickest way back into their relationship with God. That option is still the best choice for us today.

God took care of the shame of man's sin as soon as they were willing to re-open the relationship. Genesis 3:21 says, "Also for Adam and his wife the Lord God made tunics of skin, and clothed them." I have a very simple definition of <u>grace</u>: to be covered by God. It is always better to come to God first, rather than try to cope with our own sin. It naturally feels easier to <u>do something</u> for God rather than try to get to know Him. That is part of our fallen nature. Praise God, this tendency in our sin nature will be missing in heaven. God does not require us to do anything to make ourselves acceptable for this relationship. Jesus took care of everything so we don't have to. Our vulnerability is pleasing to God. He already knows what we look like under our fig leaves.

You may be asking the question: what am I expected to do? In John 6:28-29 the people asked Jesus, *"'What shall we do, that we may work the works of God?' Jesus answered and said to them, 'This is the work of God that you believe in Him whom He sent.'"* Jesus was saying that our part in the process is to <u>believe in Him</u>. It is not that you cannot do good deeds to serve others, but your motivation to do them must come from your relationship with Jesus. You can never rely on your good works as a bargaining chip to buy you favor with God. The only bargaining chip that carries clout with God is trusting in what Jesus has already done. The works you do in God's service cannot be generated from a belief in yourself or your own personal abilities. The true works of God arise out of a heart of thankfulness for what Jesus has already done. He did everything needed for salvation, now we get to live in the benefits of His finished work.

Chapter 3

What Time Period Are We In and How Do We Respond?

How do we embrace our time of engagement?

It is important as believers to understand the time period we are in so that we will be able to accurately discern God's will for our life. 1 Chronicles 12:32 says, *"of the sons of Issachar who had* <u>*understanding of the times,*</u> *to know what Israel ought to do,* their chiefs were two hundred; and all their brethren were at their command."* In this present time period of history, those of us who have accepted God's offer to spend our lives with Him are currently not married to Christ, we are engaged. We entered this engagement by being asked and saying, "Yes." It is critically important to realize that, though we are not yet married to Christ, we are one with Him through the marriage contract. The parallel of our spiritual engagement to the traditional Hebrew engagement is very revealing.

In a traditional Hebrew family, the father of the groom arranges the marriage. However, the groom still proposes to the bride and, at this time, she has the right of refusal. A bride price is paid by the groom for his bride and all of the terms of the marriage are written in a marriage contract called the "Ketubah." The Bible contains the Old and New Testaments which are covenants or contracts with God. The Old Testament (contract) was sealed with the blood of animals and provided temporary reprieve of man's sins through substitutionary animal sacrifice. The New Testament is our marriage contract sealed by the blood of Jesus. Per the terms of this contract, the permanent eradication of sin's effect was provided through the sacrifice of Jesus's life.

The "Ketubah" contains the promises that the groom has made to take care of his new wife. As you read the New Testament, it is a marriage contract and its promises are authenticated by the Groom who gave His life as the bride price. You can believe the validity of the promises based on the character of the Groom, Jesus Christ. Every promise that it contains is surer than the ground you walk on or the air you breathe because the One Who sacrificed His Life created those temporal things.

The Lord's Supper, or what is called communion, is the reminder to us of the contract. The original ceremony was called Passover and was celebrated as a memorial to the Israelites' liberation from Egypt. It was a visual image of the promised liberation that would come through Jesus, the true Passover Lamb. When Jesus ate His last earthly Passover meal with His disciples, He explained to them the true meaning of Passover. *"Likewise He also took the cup after supper, saying, 'This cup is the new covenant [contract] in My blood, which is shed for you'"* (Luke 22:20 emphasis added). There are two cups which are used to commemorate the Hebrew marriage ceremony. Jesus picked up the cup that sealed the "Ketubah" contract. Jesus will drink of the second cup at the consummation of our marriage - the Marriage Supper of the Lamb (Revelation 19:9). The cup we drink at the Lord's Supper is to remind us that we are in covenant with our groom. Jesus only drank the cup once because He never forgets His love for us, but we must drink it often so that we do not forget His love for us. 1 Corinthians 11:25 speaks about our need to remember; *"In the same manner He also took the cup after supper, saying, "This cup is the new covenant in My blood. This do, as often as you drink it, in <u>remembrance</u> of Me."*

The most important question during this time period in which we live is, "Who will accept the Ring?"

At the "Ketubah" ceremony, the bride was presented with a gift from the groom to seal the covenant. It had to be an object of value and was, customarily, a ring. The Gift Jesus gave us when we accepted His proposal was the Holy Spirit. The most important question during this time period in which we live is: "Who will accept the Ring (Holy Spirit)?" Without the Ring, there is no contract. Here is the one requirement to be a Christian: you must have the Holy Spirit. Without Him you are not in the marriage covenant (engaged). Without this Spiritual Ring there is no evidence there is a covenant between you and your Groom. The Ring seals the deal! Ephesians 1:13-14 explains this well, *"In Him you also trusted, after you heard the word of truth, the gospel of your salvation; in whom also, having believed, you were sealed with the Holy Spirit of promise, who is the guarantee of our inheritance until the redemption of the purchased possession, to the praise of His glory."* That purchased possession is you. The bride price paid for you was the life of Jesus.

To embrace our engagement, we must embrace the development of a deeper spiritual bond with Jesus. This was the purpose of the traditional Hebrew engagement period, to develop a deeper, more spiritual bond between the couple. The bride and groom were not to physically touch during the engagement period. However, they were permitted to see each other, but only in the company of a chaperon. God is not downplaying the importance of physical relations. He is only stating that the physical relationship is secondary to the spiritual bond. This parallels our present physical separation from Jesus.

When Jesus said it was better that He go away and send a Comforter, He was serious. If He were here, we would be trusting in His physical actions and His physical appearance. We would not get to know Him as well spiritually as we can now through His indwelling Spirit. I know this is difficult to believe because we think, "If I could only see Him or touch Him." However, we would not be better off. The truth is, we would cleave to His physical body and the things we could see with our eyes while not getting to know Him as well spiritually. Throughout this life on earth, it is important that the Holy Spirit guide you in your relationship with Christ because you are going to be married to Him for eternity. It is vital for you to know His motives, how He feels, and His deep love for mankind. His heart needs to be so understood that when you see Him face to face there is no fear, confusion, or nervousness on the day of the wedding.

Two of Jesus's followers did not recognized Him in a face to face conversation after His resurrection. He appeared to them while walking on a road to Emmaus. This is recorded in Luke 24:13-27. When they saw His physical body die at the cross, it was all over for them. It was not until He spoke to God in prayer that they saw Him spiritually. I believe, as Spirit indwelt believers, we would have recognized Jesus right away. They did not yet have the indwelling Holy Spirit because Jesus had not yet left the earth, releasing Him to His new assignment. Their understanding of God, from the physical aspect of Jesus, overshadowed their deeper intimacy with Him spiritually. By leaving us to return later, Jesus was doing what was in the best interest of our relationship. Everything He does for us, His bride, is in our best interest because He loves us. The knowledge of this is the foundation of your trust in Him. If you want to have great faith, then believe He loves you.

How do we cleanup for our wedding?

In the Hebrew culture there was a baptism of purification for the bride before the wedding ceremony. This <u>mikveh</u> or purification bath is one of many taken according to Hebrew spiritual traditions. This baptism in water was in order to emphasize separation or sanctification, which is the setting apart of the bride for the groom. Remember the name for the church is <u>Ecclesia</u> which means: called out or set apart. One of the first things we are commanded to do once we have made our decision to accept Jesus is to be baptized in water in His name. It is a physical sign of our declaration that we are separated from all others for Him alone. 1 Peter 3:21 says, *"The waters of baptism do that for you, not by washing away dirt from your skin but by presenting you through Jesus' resurrection before God with a clear conscience"* (MSG).

Notice, baptism is not about getting clean physically. But, how do we get the clear conscience that the scripture refers to? Is it by our work for God? No. It is by the Groom's work! You can have a clear conscience because you know that your contract is sealed by the Holy Spirit. Ephesians 4:30 says this plainly, *"And do not grieve the Holy Spirit of God, by whom you were sealed for the day of redemption."* Baptism is a way of saying thank you for choosing me. We are saying to God, I have accepted You mentally and spiritually, but I will also show You, with this physical action of baptism, that You also have my body's obedience. In short, you are declaring to God, through baptism, You have all of my love and obedience.

> ### A lot of us who love God want to help Him get the junk out of our lives.

While we are looking at baptism, I want to make a point concerning personal sanctification. How are we to keep ourselves pure for Jesus? I think the answer is found in how Jesus is relating to His church right now. Ephesians 5:25-27 gives us the understanding we need; *"Husbands, love your wives, just as Christ also loved the church and gave Himself for her, that He might sanctify and cleanse her with the washing of the water of the word, that He might present her to Himself a glorious church, not having spot or wrinkle or any such thing, that she should be holy and without blemish."* Did you notice that Jesus is the One doing the purifying and cleansing? A lot of us, who love God, want to help Him get the junk out of our lives. I know it seems logical in our rational minds to do this, but that is not what the Bible says to do.

If we cannot be cleansed or purified by our own efforts, what are we supposed to do? What we must learn to do is trust that if God can save us, He can also clean us up. We have to learn to submit ourselves to God's cleansing. Remember, God hates man's attempts to cleanse (sanctify) themselves from sin. The key to our on-going separation from sin is obedience. When I use that word, people's minds immediately shift to legalism. They may be thinking, if I obey this law, or keep this command, then I am good with God. No, it is by obeying the Voice of the Holy Spirit Who tells you what to do in any situation you may face. It is by listening to the Voice of the Holy Spirit that you can be cleansed. The sanctifying and the cleansing are accomplished in the active ongoing relationship by learning to listen and obey Love's voice. Because Jesus is your Lord, your relationship is one that requires obedience. But, is it really hard to obey if you understand that He has your best interest at heart? Once trust is developed in the relationship it is not difficult to obey Someone Who loves you.

You will never be free of trying to make yourself acceptable to God by obeying the written law. Trying not to sin is like throwing gasoline on a fire. Romans 7:8 says, *"But sin, taking opportunity by the commandment, produced in me all manner of evil desire. For apart from the law sin was dead."* If you tell yourself not to think about hot, fresh, chocolate chip cookies, then there is no doubt what you will be thinking about - hot, fresh, chocolate chip cookies. You must learn to relax and follow the voice of the Holy Spirit to be cleansed by Him. You have the Living Seal of your covenant with God on the inside of you, and He is there to help you with your relationship to God. Jesus said, *"…and I will pray the father, and He will give you another helper, that he may abide with you forever"* (John 14:16). Just like an earthly wedding ring guides you in your marriage relationship, the Holy Spirit your living Ring, guides you in your eternal relationship.

***If God brought us into relationship with Him through a new birth,
then He loves us enough to clean us up.***

As I was struggling with how to best teach this truth, I asked God about this principle of Him doing the work of cleansing us. You see, this is not the world's system. In the world's system everything is generated by our effort and determination, otherwise known as "willpower." I said, "God I don't know how to teach this. Give me a picture." Immediately, in my mind, I saw a cow cleaning the mucus off of her new-born calf by licking it. And God said to me, "Son, don't you think that I love them as much as that dumb cow loves her calf?"

If God united us with Him through the new birth, then He certainly loves us enough to clean us up after we are born again. All we have to do is be obedient and let Him do the work. Please, stop trying to get yourself cleaned up. Just relax and listen to the Voice of your Bridegroom through His indwelling Spirit. He has your best interest at heart every single time. If you believe what I am telling you, then the great news is that you can lighten up. God never seems to be in a hurry! Understanding God's perspective on eternity destroys our anxious thoughts of quickly completing our spiritual journey.

How sure is Christ's return?

The price paid for your hand in marriage was so exorbitant, there is no possibility that Jesus will not return to earth to get His purchased bride. The returning of Jesus Christ is the surest thing in this universe! We may not know the day or the hour, but with absolute certainty He will come! *"For the Lord Himself will descend from heaven with a shout, with the voice of an archangel, and the trumpet of God. And the dead in Christ will rise first. Then we who are alive and remain shall be caught up together with them in the clouds to meet the Lord in the air. And thus we shall always be with the Lord"* (1 Thessalonians 4:16-17).

In Hebrew culture, the bridegroom left after the signing of the "Ketubah" to make preparations for his future wife. The preparations included building a place for the couple to live, which was typically an addition onto the house of the groom's father. Listen to Jesus's words about this: *"<u>In my Father's house</u> are many mansions. If it were not so, I would have told you. I go to prepare a place for you, and if I go and prepare a place for you, I will come again and receive you to myself that where I am, there you may be also" (John 14:2-3).* Everything you may have heard about having a mansion in heaven one day cannot compare to the truth. You will live in the house of God in heaven.

If the Son of God has been preparing a place for me for 2000 years, what does that look like?

I cannot explain how relational heaven will be! We cannot even fathom how close we will be with God. We will have the complete understanding that God has about our brothers and sisters in Christ. We will know each other's hearts without the presence of sin. Talk about a good time! No matter what happens here on earth during our lifetime, it is a trivial amount of time compared to eternity.

If our assignment here on earth is to deepen our relationship with God spiritually, then what are Jesus's responsibilities while He is in Heaven? Is He merely sitting on a throne waiting for us? It says in John 14:2 that He is preparing a place for us. If the Son of God has been preparing a place for me for 2000 years what does that look like? In my mind, I have no way to comprehend what Jesus is <u>preparing</u>.

I have shown you that at the end of our time here on earth, we will be united with the Son in marriage. At this time, our ultimate destiny will finally be fulfilled. Our destiny is Jesus lavishing His love on us, His bride, for all of eternity. If Jesus's ministry as a Bridegroom is glorious, then what does the Bible say His ministry as a Husband will be like? *"Eye has not seen, nor ear heard, nor has entered into the heart of man, the things which God has prepared for those who love Him" (1 Corinthians 2:9).*

Chapter 4

If We Were Rescued, Why Were We Left On Earth?

What was Jesus's rescue mission?

Jesus's mission was to rescue His bride. How did He accomplish His mission? The only begotten Son of God came to earth as a helpless baby, lived a sinless life and, by His character and accompanying actions, accurately demonstrated for everyone exactly what God is really like. When the time came to implement the rescue mission, Jesus, who is also the Commander of the armies of heaven, did not use the power at His command, but implemented the rescue alone. He permitted Himself to be captured knowing all of His followers would flee, thereby lovingly protecting all of them. Jesus said in John 17:12, *"While I was with them in the world, I kept them in your name. Those whom You gave Me I have kept; and none of them is lost except the son of perdition, that the scripture might be fulfilled."*

To allow yourself to be captured, tortured, and killed, in order to have the ability to set the one you love free, is the greatest example of self-sacrificial love that the world has ever seen.

After Jesus allowed His capture, He consented to torture while, at any point, He could have called in reinforcements. Jesus clearly explains this to one of His disciples in Matthew 26:52-53: *"Put your sword in its place, for all who take the sword die by the sword. Or do you think that I cannot now pray to My Father, and He will provide me with more than twelve legions of angels?"* After being tortured for nearly a full day, Jesus was led away to be killed by the brutal method of crucifixion. He embraced crucifixion as the means to gain access to Hades where the dead were being held captive by Satan. *"Therefore He says, 'When He ascended on high, He led captivity captive, And gave gifts to men.' (Now this, "He ascended" — what does it mean but that He also first descended into the lower parts of the earth? He who descended is also the One who ascended far above all the heavens, that He might fill all things)"* (Ephesians 4:8-10).

Because Jesus had been unjustly condemned (having no sin in Him), the devil was unable to control Jesus's actions. By the power of the Holy Spirit, Jesus was raised from the dead thereby completely striping the devil of the authority he possessed over mankind since his deception of them in the Garden of Eden. The devil had previously held the power to invoke the death penalty because it was the just sentence for man's sin. *"For the wages of sin is death, but the gift of God is eternal life in Jesus Christ our Lord"* (Romans 6:23). This was because man had obeyed the devil instead of God, thereby making the devil their lord with the accompanying authority to enforce the penalty of sin. Through Jesus's resurrection from the dead, He usurped the devil's authority to enforce judgment. Hebrews 2:14

says it this way, *"Inasmuch then as the children have partaken of flesh and blood, He [Jesus] Himself likewise shared in the same, that through death He might destroy him who had the power of death, that is, the devil."*

To allow yourself to be captured, tortured, and killed in order to have the ability to set the one you love free, is the greatest example of self-sacrificial love that the world has ever seen. Jesus's love for His bride, who was taken captive, is irrefutable. What makes Jesus's selfless action even nobler is the reality that there was no guarantee that anyone would accept His proposal. Remember that in His darkest hour, none of His followers had stood by Him. He sacrificed everything without knowing if even one person would accept His proposal.

I want to ask you a question to make an important point. Who aided Jesus with this rescue mission? No one! The most brilliant plan ever conceived to defeat an enemy was carried out by one lone Soldier, as a man, without utilizing His heavenly authority. Who then deserves the credit for setting the human race free? <u>Jesus Christ alone.</u> This honor and distinction is held by no one other than Jesus, our Bridegroom.

Why was the church left on earth?

The main reason you were left on earth was to deepen your spiritual intimacy with the Bridegroom before the wedding.

If I ask almost any Christian why the church was left on earth, ninety percent of the time the answer will be to win the lost. Now, while that is a good answer, I want to show you from the Bible that there is more to it than that. The main reason you were left on earth was to develop your spiritual intimacy with the Bridegroom before the wedding. The result of this spiritual intimacy is that more people will come to know God. Here is a simple analogy. How do two people produce a baby? It is through intimacy. If intimacy is God's plan for reproduction, then how are we going to reproduce a baby Christian without first becoming intimate with God?

I am not questioning the heart of any brother or sister in Christ. But, my purpose is to expose this fundamental truth: Satan is patient. He attempts, over time, to strategically shift our focus away from intimacy with God. *"Lest Satan should take advantage of us; for we are not ignorant of his devices" (2 Corinthians 2:11).* The shift of focus from an intimate relationship with God to activities performed for God has created superficiality in the church. This superficiality is unable to reproduce the relational heart of God. I believe the resulting lack of knowledge of our heavenly Father's character is the key contributor to the apathy in the present day church. This apathy further perpetuates the perception that intimacy with God is not necessary. Intimacy is not only necessary, it is to be the foundation for our entire Christian experience. God is always relational. Any strategy that destroys our relationship with Him originates from the devil.

When well-meaning Christians try to go out and reproduce without intimacy with God, it is as if they are reproducing through the artificial insemination of their religious works. The new Christian can be a true born again believer, but still be confused about what their Daddy is like. Since children copy what they see their parents do, the cycle keeps repeating itself. There are millions of Christians reproduced this way who have no idea what their heavenly Father is really like.

I said earlier that we are God's favorite subject. That is a bold statement, but I know it is true. God loves people. If we become intimate with God, we will develop His heart for people. God's desire is to include everyone in the upcoming marriage. When we begin to feel the heartbeat of God we begin to see people the way He sees them. God cares about the nations. Psalm 2:8 says, *"Ask of Me, and I will give you the nations for your inheritance."* Does this mean God cares about geographical countries? No! He cares about the people in those countries. With God's heart we will influence people to draw near to Him; without His heart, our influence is limited to our own abilities. 1 Corinthians 13:1 says that without love we, *"…become like sounding brass or a clanging symbol."* Our works, without the motive of love, are simply not as effective.

Spiritual intimacy is the key to the almost effortless fulfillment of the great commission.

But, what about Jesus's great commission in Matthew 28:19-20? *"Go therefore and make disciples of all the nations, baptizing them in the name of the Father and of the Son and of the Holy Spirit, teaching them to observe all things that I have commanded you; and lo, I am with you always, even to the end of the age."* I will clearly show you, from the Bible, that spiritual intimacy is the key to the almost effortless fulfillment of the great commission. It was never meant to be a toiling labor like Adam experienced after the fall of man. It was meant to be done with joy from the heart.

A passage in the Song of Solomon is the clearest example of this truth. In short, here is the story line. This is about the Shulamite, the bride-to-be of King Solomon (Song of Solomon 5:2-6:1). She is in bed for the night, has taken her makeup off, and put her nightgown on. When Solomon comes to the door, she is not ready to receive visitors and does not go to the door right away. She changes her mind, but it is too late; he is gone.

> *"I sleep, but my heart is awake; it is the voice of my beloved! He knocks, saying, "open for me, my sister, my love, my dove, my perfect one; for my head is covered with dew, my locks with the drops of the night." I have taken off my robe; how can I put it on again? I have washed my feet; how can I defile them? My beloved put his hand by the latch of the door, and my heart yearned for him. I arose to open for my beloved, and my hands dripped with myrrh, my fingers with liquid myrrh, on the handles of the lock. I opened for my beloved, but my beloved had turned away and was gone. My heart leaped up when he spoke. I sought him, but I could not find him; I called him, but he gave no answer" (5:2-6).*

After Solomon departs, the Shulamite goes searching for him. Getting harassed by the local authorities in the process, she solicits other ladies in the town to help her find him.

> *"The watchmen who went about the city found me. They struck me, they wounded me; the keepers of the walls took my veil away from me. I charge you O daughters of Jerusalem if you find my beloved, that you tell him I am lovesick" (5:7-6:1).*

The ladies then ask the Shulamite what makes her man so special.

> *"What is your beloved more than another beloved, O fairest among women? What is your beloved more than another beloved, that you so charge us?" (5:9).*

They earnestly want to know what could possibly be so great about her man that would cause her to pursue him so passionately. Notice that they ask her about the one she loves. Here is her reply:

> "My beloved is white and ruddy, chief among ten thousand. His head is like the finest gold; his locks are wavy, and black as a raven. His eyes are like doves by the rivers of waters, washed with milk, and fitly set. His cheeks are like a bed of spices, banks of scented herbs. His lips are lilies, dripping liquid myrrh. His hands are rods of gold set with beryl. His body is carved ivory inlaid with sapphires. His legs are pillars of marble set on bases of fine gold. His countenance is like Lebanon, excellent as the cedars. His mouth is most sweet, yes, he is altogether lovely. This is my beloved, and this is my friend, O daughters of Jerusalem!" (5:10-16).

Remember these ladies were totally indifferent in the beginning, but are now questioning her. Listen to their response to her description, "Where has your beloved gone, O fairest among women? Where has your beloved turned aside, that we may seek him with you?" (Song of Solomon 6:1). Do you see the change in their hearts toward the one that she loves?

Your passion to follow God at any cost is very attractive. People will want the relationship you have.

This is how the great commission is fulfilled – falling so in love with the Bridegroom you must seek Him and share Him with others. When someone asks you why you are so in love, you simply tell them about Jesus. This is how it is supposed to flow;

not doing work for God, but sharing your relationship with God. Love for God results in what He desires: your heart to be one with His heart. What is God passionate about? God passionately cares about people. The more intimately you are connected with God by His Spirit living in you, guiding you, and teaching you; the more you know His heart. The more you know His heart, the more His heart is part of your everyday interaction. Just like the Shulamite, even if you are wandering around, harassed on every side, beaten, and your possessions taken; your love will compel you to pursue Him.

Your passion to follow God at any cost is very attractive to others. People will want what you have. This is God's plan for the church during the engagement period. The early church had this type of respect from the world. *"Yet none of the rest dared join them, but the people esteemed them highly" (Acts 5:13).* Even people who will not agree with your beliefs will respect your commitment when it is out of a love relationship with God.

I want to give an analogy that explains how spiritual reproduction works in everyday life. What naturally happens after you go to a great restaurant and experience the combination of great food and great service? You tell people about the restaurant; you even rave about it because you are now a fan. Then you take it a step further, you look for ways to bring up the restaurant in conversation. The same analogy applies to a great movie. Some movies, with very limited advertising budgets, have gone on to sell a lot more tickets and video rentals through this word-of-mouth method. The concept of having passion for something before you share it is just how the human heart was designed to function. A successful salesman must believe in his product first or he is just a hustler, operating solely for his own interest. None of us likes to be sold anything, but when the person really loves their product and believes it could help us, then we will listen. Their motive is no longer selfish, they are sharing something they personally believe would be beneficial to us.

How is our engagement different from the marriage?

If we are not yet united to Christ completely, as we would consider a marriage that's consummated, what will be the difference once we are? Please look at **Diagram A** once again. We, who have accepted Christ, are now one in the Son by the marriage contract, but if you will look at eternity future, you will see we continue to be one in the Son. What does the Bible declare happens to two people once they are married? It says that they become one flesh. Ephesians 5:31-32 makes it very clear, *"For this reason a man shall leave his father and mother and be joined to his wife, and the two shall become one flesh. This is a great mystery, but I speak concerning Christ and the church."* Paul makes it clear that the covenant of marriage on the earth is also a picture of the heavenly marriage of Christ and His church.

From the beginning, the Gospel plan has been to unite us in a marriage relationship with the Son of God.

I have a question for you, and the answer is almost impossible to believe. If two married people become one, in regards to your union with Christ, where does that put you in the future? If you are one with the Son, who is God, then you are united in God forever. When I said the bigger picture of the gospel was grander than most Christians can even imagine, I was not exaggerating. This is the full magnitude of the gospel. From the beginning, the gospel plan has been to unite us in a marriage relationship with the Son of God. According to Ephesians 1:3-4 that has always been God's plan. *"Blessed be the God and Father of our Lord Jesus Christ, who has blessed us with every spiritual blessing in the heavenly places in Christ, just as He chose us in Him before the foundation of the world, that we should be holy and without blame before Him in love."* Not only did God rescue us out of the horrible grip of sin, but He restored us so that our original destiny could be fulfilled.

Is this a man-centered gospel?

"Who gets more attention at a wedding, the bride or the groom?"

The gospel is almost too much for us to grasp. Though we may have grown up in church, most of us have never heard the magnitude of God's plan. If you have heard this before, it may still be difficult to process because it is so humbling. Most everything that I have spoken about so far has centered on mankind. Can that really be how it is? I was struggling with the concept of what was appearing to be a man-centered gospel, and these thoughts were in a prayer to God. While this was happening, God asked me two questions that really helped me. The first was, "What do you think it looks like from My perspective?" You see, to God it is all about us. Love's focus is on the object of His affection and we are the object of His love. From God's perspective, it is a man-centered gospel.

The second question made everything very clear to me, "Who gets more attention at a wedding, the bride or the groom?" The groom is hardly thought about at all, yet isn't he the real hero? He is the one promising to take care of the bride for the rest of her life. He is the key to everything, but as a servant leader, he has made the focus of his love the bride. It is the same way with Jesus. The price He paid is staggering, but we are the focus of all His effort. Remember the song earlier, "The One You Love." God wanted me to share those lyrics with people in order to change how they perceive their worth. He wants us to understand the significance of our value to Him.

I am worth the life of Jesus Christ.

If I had a used car listed for sale at $5,000, what is the car worth? I am not sure yet because it is only worth what someone will pay for it. Maybe I'll get $4,800 or maybe $4,500. Worth is determined by the buyer, not the seller. God bought you at a price, and that price was the life of Jesus Christ. Now here is the most humbling question you will ever answer if you will speak the truth and not your feelings. What are you worth? Can you even say it? Keep in mind, something is worth what the buyer is willing to pay. It is not worth what the seller or even the item considers itself to be worth. Read it with me and then I want you to say it out loud. I am worth the life of Jesus Christ. Now say it out loud. I am worth the life of Jesus Christ. Understanding your worth does not make you proud; it causes you to glorify God Who not only set your price, but paid it. *"Or do you not know that your body is the temple of the Holy Spirit who is in you, whom you have from God, and you are not your own? For you were <u>bought at a price</u>; therefore glorify God in your body and in your spirit, which are God's"* (1 Corinthians 1:19-20).

Chapter 5

How Do I Walk Into My Destiny?

How do I fight the lie of introspection?

My objective is to make it extremely clear what thoughts should be submitted to and what thoughts should be resisted. Once they are brought into the open, my hope is that you will choose to terminate their negative influence in your life. *"Therefore, submit to God, resist the devil and he will flee from you" (James 4:7).* I have been criticized by well-meaning people who tell me I should not be so introspective. I am not dwelling on the negative for self-analysis; I am exposing the lies so they can be recognized. I would like to talk to you about your future, but my focus will be on what is opposing the fulfillment of your destiny.

You are caught in the middle of a spiritual war. Whether you believe it or not does not change that fact.

Only the devil would be deceptive enough to tell you to just focus on the positive. This, of course, keeps everyone's eyes off his attacks against us. This is like an enemy telling you not to look behind you while he stabs you in the back. Let me make this very clear: you are caught in the middle of a spiritual war. Whether you believe it or not does not change that fact. Don't ever forget, you are what all of creation was made for. You are worth the life of Jesus. No matter how you feel about it, you are extremely valuable. You are worth fighting over, period! All I am doing is exposing the strategies of the devil's assault against you.

How does God's kingdom expand?

If we get the order right (intimacy first), children come naturally.

We have seen that reproduction on earth is through intimacy. God's spiritual kingdom is reproduced in the same way: intimate relationship. But practically, what does this look like? Do you realize what you are doing at this very moment in time? You are pursuing a deeper intimacy with God by choosing to read this book about your relationship with Him. The intimacy you gain, through the Holy Spirit revealing something in these pages, will reproduce. This is why your relationship with God is constantly under attack. When you spend time with God, it produces positive results. The Shulamite in the Song of Solomon got it right – intimacy first! Out of that place of intimacy children come naturally.

I have heard a lot of teaching about how we should return to the book of Acts and <u>do</u> what the early church <u>did</u>. The strength of the early church was the relationship they had with Jesus. The motive behind their actions was their knowledge of His love for them. They saw Him die for them and be raised from the dead. They knew, beyond a shadow of a doubt, that Jesus cared passionately about them. When they told others about Jesus it was not a sales pitch; it was a love story. Out of their reciprocating love for Jesus came the conviction and passion that changed the world – The Acts of the Apostles.

How can we understand the faith of the early church? Hebrews 11:6, says, *"But without faith it is impossible to please Him, for he who comes to God must believe that He is, and that He is a rewarder of those who diligently seek Him."* The word <u>rewarder</u> means <u>remunerator</u> which defined is: to pay in like kind. This concerned me because it appeared to sound like working to earn God's approval. This is how this actually plays out in our relationship with God. The extent to which we are determined to pursue God is the extent to which we will receive more of Him in return. If we chase Him for two miles, we get two miles worth of intimacy, revelation, and understanding. If we chase Him ten miles, we get ten miles worth. This is how faith works.

At first this may seem like works, but it is simply passion from our heart. God answers passion with revelation from His heart which in turn develops more passion. But, without pursuit, the enemy will steal what you have already gained. *"For I say to you, that to everyone who has will be given; and from him who does not have, even what he has will be taken away from him" (Luke 19:26).* It is impossible to stay neutral in your relationship with God. God loathes a lukewarm heart. *"I know your works, that you are neither cold nor hot. I could wish you were cold or hot. So then, because you are lukewarm, and neither cold nor hot, I will vomit you out of my mouth" (Revelation 3:15-16).*

If we want to be like the early church, we have to stir up our hearts to accept, like they did, the overwhelming love of Jesus. On this critical point of love I feel a very fundamental mistake can sometimes be made. We often concentrate our focus on how much we love God. Be careful. It is more prudent to think about how much God loves you and the resulting by-product will be: you love God. Your worth comes from who loves you, not how much love you can produce. Satan will attempt to turn the focus of your love for God into a self-righteous work. If you catch yourself measuring your love for God, you have fallen into this trap. I personally believe it is more beneficial, in the development of your relationship with God, to dwell on His love for you. A practical way to do this is to mainly let the songs you listen to and sing focus on God's love for you, and not your love for God. Warning! Don't become the song police, just try this for yourself and experience the results.

How does Satan undermine our worship of God?

What is God's motivation for desiring our worship of Him?

Worship is such an intimate part of our relationship with God that Satan will attempt to undermine our desire for worship. One way he does this is by planting false ideas about why God desires worship. Satan is often able to deceive us because, through our human weakness, we believe God thinks like we think. This is not true! *"For My thoughts are not your thoughts, nor are your ways My ways, says the Lord. For as the heavens are higher than the earth, so are My ways higher than your ways, and My thoughts than Your thoughts"* (Isaiah 55:8). In Hebrew the word <u>thoughts</u> means: intentions or plans. This is referring to God's motives. The word <u>ways</u> means: course of life or mode of action. This is referring to what action God will take. Both

God's motives and actions are above the motives and actions of our fallen nature. Thank God we can renew our mind!

What is God's motivation for desiring our worship of Him? If your explanation makes God seem vain or insecure in any way, Satan has deceived you by using the above strategy. Remember from 1 Corinthians 13:5 that love does not seek its own. Therefore, it is impossible for God (Who is Love) to be the One who needs worship. God does not desire worship for any of the same reasons we would desire worship. His motivations are higher than our motivations. God's motive for desiring worship is completely for our benefit! Jesus, Who is God, contrasted His heart with Satan's heart in John 10:10: *"The thief does not come except to steal, and to kill, and to destroy. I have come that they may have life, and that they may have it more abundantly."* God's desire is that we have **life** and have it abundantly, but what does that have to do with God's motive for worshiping Him? Everything! Jesus said in John 14:6, *"I am the way, the truth, and **the life**. No one comes to the Father except through Me."*

God desires for you to worship Him out of the totally selfless motivation of you receiving a blessing.

God is not like an earthly father who could desire praise because He is vain or insecure. God is Life Himself. God wants you to have abundant life, but the only way for you to have Life is to come to Him, because He is The Life. God desires for you to worship Him out of the totally selfless motivation of you receiving a blessing. That blessing is Himself. To accurately describe what happens in worship I must quote a Beatles song. "All you need is love, love, love is all you need."[A] What happens in worship is you receive what you actually need: Love. Whether you realize it or not, Love is all you need. *"And* we have known and believed the love that God had for us. God is love, and he who abides in love, abides in God, and God in him" (I John 4:16).

Am I saying that God gets nothing out of worship? Absolutely not! God receives a joy greater than someone who just gave a gift to a friend which they had been desiring for a long time. God is elated that you are receiving His Love as you worship and He is thrilled that this is what you want and desperately need. The <u>higher motivation</u> of God is that He was only thinking about you getting the gift. A selfish thought has never entered into the mind of God. That is an impossibility.

Satan is only able to get us to think this way because we have operated out of our <u>lower selfish thoughts</u> for so long, but we are no longer ignorant of his schemes (1 Corinthians 2:11). Thank God our heads have been lifted to a new place by the power of the indwelling Holy Spirit! *"For who has known the mind of the Lord that he may instruct Him? But we have the mind of Christ"* (1 Corinthians 2:16). Now you can come to worship knowing that God's only thought is you, and the longings of your heart, both perceived and unperceived, will be filled. Every motive God has is Holy. No longer be deceived by Satan who is unable to comprehend the selfless motivations of God.

Who is the perfect example of reproduction?

David is a perfect example of how we reproduce the heart of God. As a small boy keeping his father's sheep, David had become accustomed to worshipping God on his lyre as he would sing to the sheep. The intimacy he experienced with God was remunerated, or paid back by God to David, in the understanding of God's heart. This caused David to care like God did. David cared enough to protect the sheep at the risk of his own life. David's passion, even as a young boy, gave him the strength to kill a lion and a bear in order to deliver his father's sheep from their enemies.

That day on a hillside in Israel, the heart of a boy and His God were one.

Passion often manifests itself in a fearless trust in the one who loves you. David so trusted God and the promises of His covenant that he was absolutely fearless when he fought and killed a giant named Goliath. He even told Goliath what he would do to him before they started to fight. *"This day the Lord will deliver you into my hand, and I will strike you and take your head from you… Then all this assembly shall know that the Lord does not save with sword and spear; for the battle is the Lord's, and He will give you into our hands"* (1 Samuel 17:46,47). We see clearly from his own words that David was not relying on his own strength, but God's strength. God used His heart of deliverance, which David had passionately received through intimacy, to save Israel. That day on a hillside in Israel, the heart of a boy and His God were one.

Observe the results of David's oneness with God: God's enemies were destroyed and His people were freed from fear. Because David had pursued intimacy with God, Goliath was as good as dead when he woke up that morning. Goliath made it his goal to mock God and His covenant people every day he came to the battlefield, yet no one would dispute his lies. On this particular day, a boy was present who intimately knew his God and could not tolerate the lies about the character of his heavenly Father. God rewarded David's intimacy with His Deliverer's heart. God's love had delivered David from fear. David reproduced that same fearlessness in his fellow Hebrew soldiers who, that day, delivered their nation. People who are freed from the grip of lies have the ability to lead others to that same place of freedom.

David's destiny, as a leader of Israel, was established as a result of his intimacy with God. This is the same way your destiny will be established. Your future is so tied into God you will never discover it without pursuing Him. David received the greatest commendation that God has ever paid a man. This is how the prophet Samuel described David, the next King of Israel, to Saul, the then current king: *"The Lord has sought for Himself <u>a man after His own heart</u>, and the Lord has commanded him to be commander over His people, because you have not kept what the Lord commanded you"* *(1 Samuel 13:14)*.

The passion of an intimate relationship will produce a militant attitude, which is what we are witnessing in the story of David and Goliath. For example, if someone I didn't know was unjustly attacked, I would become offended at the injustice, but if one of my children were attacked, I would become outraged. The passion to protect becomes so fierce because I would be going beyond what was best for me personally. I would not be thinking about my personal safety; I would not be thinking of myself at all, only about the one I love. Unlike the soldiers, who tolerated the lies of Goliath as he mocked their God, David knew God personally; therefore, he defended the attack against Him. This is the level of passion that Christ entered into as He executed His plan to rescue you from His enemy, the devil. That is why it is referred to as "The Passion of Christ." When passion is in your heart toward God, you are invincible. Satan, at all cost, must attempt to thwart your intimacy with God.

What makes mankind so special?

The relational aspect of the human heart is how you are most like your Creator.

Let's look at what makes mankind the pinnacle of God's creation. Turn to Jeremiah 29:11, and I want you to notice something in this passage that talks about your future. It says, *"For I know the thoughts that I think toward you, says the Lord, thoughts of peace and not of evil, to give you a future and a hope."* Although I was very familiar with this passage, I had not noticed that it says God will give you a future. I asked God, "How do You do that?" Over time He revealed to me how our future is brought to pass.

Genesis 1:27 tells us that God made man (us) in His own image. Since we know God is love (I John 4:16), He created us to have the ability to live in loving relationships with others. He created in us a heart that desires relationship. However, another significant quality of being made in God's image is our ability to first imagine and then create. It is through our unique, imaginative personality that God will influence the maximum number of people. This is a distinctively unique place where we will find genuine fulfillment.

I experience being in this distinctive place when I teach a group of people who are hungry to know God. This is where I enter into agreement with God, and the words He is giving me to say are making an impact in the lives of those in the audience. Sometimes in those moments I will be teaching revelations on the character of God which I have never heard before. I believe David was experiencing this place of agreement with God as he told Goliath what was about to happen to him. You have a distinctive place where you enter into agreement with God, and my desire is to show you how to find it.

If anything happens for good on this planet, it has to come out of the heart of a man or a women.

Ephesians 1:15-18 is part of Paul's prayer for the church in Ephesus:

> *"Therefore I also, after I heard of your faith in the Lord*
> *Jesus and your love for all the saints, do not cease*
> *to give thanks for you, making mention of you in my*
> *prayers: that the God of our Lord Jesus Christ, the*
> *Father of glory, may give to you the spirit of wisdom*
> *and revelation in the knowledge of Him, that the eyes*
> *of your understanding being enlightened that you may*
> *know what is the hope of His calling, what are the*
> *riches of the glory of His inheritance in the saints."*

Where are <u>the riches of the glory of His inheritance</u>? It says they are in the saints. Saints is a term used to refer to all believers in God through Jesus. You may have never thought to ask yourself this question, but its understanding is essential. If anything good happens on this earth, how does it happen?

I feel relatively sure that a group of whales is not meeting together at this moment in the Pacific Ocean for the purpose of solving world hunger. The reason these whales are not meeting to solve this problem is because if anything good happens on this planet, it has to come out of the heart of a man or a woman. Everything of lasting significance in this world originates from inside people. There are people who have been used by God to accomplish great things. However, the reason the verse says <u>in the Saints</u> is because only those people who are yielded to God can accomplish His purposes <u>and</u> bring Him glory through their lives.

God gives you your future by first showing you a picture in your imagination. The riches in you are going to come out through the creative imagination that God has given you. God will give you an idea or an image in your mind of how something could look, or how it could be improved. Then, in an act of childlike trust, you must believe your heavenly Father will bring it to pass. Jesus said in Luke 18:17, *"Assuredly, I say to you, whoever does not receive the kingdom of God as a little child will by no means enter it."* Isn't it interesting that one of the first things a child usually loses on their way to adolescence is their imagination? That is not a coincidence! It is a strategic plan of Satan. Remember, anything good that happens on this earth comes out of the heart of a man or woman. If the key to bringing out the good in us is the imagination then, by necessity, it will be a primary target of our enemy.

Is there anyone just like me?

For the first time in my life I understood that everyone is not just different, they are different on purpose.

In the spring of 2010 during a worship service, I had some thoughts which seemed out of place for a worship service. In truth, at the time, this did not seem all that spiritual. While the music was playing, I began to contemplate how different people are as individuals. I had thought about this previously, but in this moment my mind was concentrated on our individuality. As I considered the six billion people on earth and the truth that no two of them are identical, I was in awe of God's ability. A holy reverence came over me when I realized the significance of no two people being identical. I understood in my heart that there was a reason for our individuality, but I was receiving God's perspective about our uniqueness. For the first time in my life I understood that everyone is not just different, they are different on purpose.

While in this state of mind I began to imagine the amount of information that would be needed to create a person. I was envisioning this information in a single line and wondering how long the line would need to be to contain all the information required to create a person. At the same time, I pictured a teaching illustration to show how different we are from one another. I pictured two lines comparing two unique individuals. What I was really focusing on was how to show or demonstrate individual uniqueness. I could picture two lines of information on strings extending out of the building and by measuring the two lines I could accurately demonstrate individual uniqueness. I assumed the lines would be several miles long and was excited about this awesome illustration.

I am about to give you a lot of numbers that will help you understand your uniqueness. I began researching and discovered that there are thirty thousand genes in the human genome with about one million characters in each, totaling thirty billion characters in the human genome. This gave me the number of bits of information needed to create a person, which was what I had been picturing during worship.

I soon discovered that as recently as ten years ago a discovery had been made that rendered previous estimates of human differences totally inaccurate. Scientist had previously taken a like gene from individuals or primates to compare that same gene. With this method it was determined that all humans were 99.9 percent alike and that humans had 99 percent of gene compatibility with primates. A glaring mistake had been made, however, by not taking into consideration the difference in the overall gene count of each individual, which can vary greatly. While the individual gene might have been similar, the total number of that same gene for each person was not. Of a particular gene, one person could have a total of thirty while another a total of two hundred and fifty. With this broader perspective in mind, it is now estimated that the difference between every person on the planet varies as much as 10-12 percent. That is over 1000 percent more than previously thought. With this newly discovered information I proceeded to calculate the length of the lines needed to create individuals.

The line of information that would be needed to build an individual person at a size 10 font with no spaces is 3,192 miles long, or roughly 5,000 kilometers. This would be equivalent to drawing a line from Maine to Seattle, WA. If this information was converted to book format it would be 145,000 pages with no spaces. To give you a perspective, this would be equivalent to 145 one thousand page books. The Bible speaks about the personal touch of our creator on all of us. Psalm 139:13-14 says, *"For You formed my inward parts; You covered me in my mother's womb. I will praise You, for I am fearfully and wonderfully made; marvelous are Your works, and that my soul knows very well."* But, what about the two lines that I saw showing the differences between individual people?

The measurable difference between you and anyone else is 10-12 percent of our original calculations. There are 319 miles of information which are uniquely yours alone. In book format that is the equivalent of 14,500 pages that are only written about you. Multiply that number by six billion and you will be in awe of the greatness of our God. This should elevate your understanding of how important each one of us is to God. A quote from one of the scientific journals on the internet always makes me laugh, "Significantly more variation exists than previously thought. Questions will be raised as to whose genome will be considered normal."[B] Accounting for all of the people on earth, no two are exactly alike. Every single person is an original creation without a "normal" standard. Our conclusion must be that the uniqueness of each individual is on purpose, but why does this matter?

> *"Be yourself; everything else is just a copy; I don't make copies, only originals."*

If your individual uniqueness is on purpose wouldn't it stand to reason that your individuality might be the key to finding your destiny? God desires you to be free to be who He created you to be; He is not interested in you copying anyone else. In the car one morning, God explained this to me clearly. He said, "Be yourself; everything else is just a copy; I don't make copies, only originals." I knew this was God speaking because the meaning of what he said permeated through all His creation. The first thing that went through my mind was that no two snowflakes are exactly alike. Then I realized that nothing in the whole of creation is an exact duplicate. Everything God creates is an original. Satan is aware of the danger of your originality coming out. One of his strategies will be to provoke you into comparison for the sole purpose of stopping your individuality. We will be discussing this in greater depth in Chapter 13.

[A] "All You Need Is Love", Lennon-McCartney, 1967
[B] www.bionews.org

Chapter 6

How Do I Hold Onto God's Vision For My Life?

How can your vision be stolen?

God loves you and wants to give you a future. Satan is afraid of anyone who understands the knowledge of the love of God in their heart and dares to believe the unique dreams that God gives them. The only truly satisfying future is one that is in agreement with the purposes of God. Philippians 2:13 says, *"It is God that works in you, both to will and to do of his good pleasure."* A creative unity emerges between you and God in which He gives you a glimpse of your future and you begin to believe that He can bring it to pass. For many people this vision is stolen by Satan before it can be firmly planted in their heart. Satan is concerned about your ability to bring God's vision for your life to pass through the developing trust in your relationship with Him.

The first attack against your destiny is the attempt to steal God's vision. In Habakkuk 2:2 God tells His prophet to, *"Write the*

vision and make it plain on tablets, that he may run who reads it."
God states plainly that with a clear vision people are able to run
forward. In Habakkuk 2:3 God even says a clear vision can impart
the patience you will need until it comes to pass. *"For the vision is
yet for an appointed time; but at the end it will speak, and it will
not lie. Though it tarries, wait for it; because it will surely come, it
will not tarry."*

Don't be afraid to ask God to restore His vision for you.

Some of you have had God's vision for your future stolen. It might
have been so long ago, that you cannot even remember the dreams
and desires of your heart. God, Who is Love, hopes all things and
believes all things. Don't be afraid to ask God to restore His vision for
you. The key will be to faithfully obey the vision He shares from this
present moment forward. It will be difficult not to look at the time
that may have been stolen along the way, but I would encourage
you to resist feelings of regret and/or failure. God never sees you as
a failure. It is impossible for Him to think of you as a failure because
He hopes all things for you and believes all things about you.

There is a story in the Old Testament about Solomon's temple
being rebuilt in Jerusalem. On the joyous day of the temple's
dedication, after years of construction, the older people lamented
because they remembered the grandeur of the previous temple.
The demonic trap of comparison had stolen their joy. The younger
people, who had not seen the former temple, were joyful for what
God was doing in the present moment. The key is to not compare
your former life to your current life, or even your future life. Only
ask God to make His vision clear and be grateful when He speaks
to you. I will be explaining later in this chapter who is responsible

for bringing the vision to pass. You only need to believe God is able; after all, He is God. He is fully aware of how much time you have left on the earth. In this chapter we will be looking at Moses as an example of someone who got his eyes off of God and onto himself due to time and circumstances. Keep your eyes on God; He is Able! When God shows you a vision, with your cooperation, He will bring it to pass.

How do I interpret God's vision for my future?

It has been my observation that God may reveal certain aspects of your future based on your personality. For most of my life, I have been too aggressive in decision making. When God has shown me just a partial glimpse of my future, I have tried to bring it to pass in my own strength, many times with disastrous results. As I get older I am understanding what Habakkuk meant about the vision being for an appointed time.

There are other personality types who make decisions more slowly. This thoughtfulness can be a great asset, but if the delay is motivated by fear, God is not pleased when fear is chosen over trusting Him. The weakness of the aggressive personality is to trust in themselves, while the weakness of the passive personality is to fail to trust God. Both of these weaknesses can be equally damaging to seeing the vision come to pass.

Here are some practical examples of how this works. A God inspired idea of helping foster children may well up in your heart, and the longer you visualize the idea you begin imagining solutions to improve the children's lives. Or, God may inspire a vision of a work of art that could stir the inner longings of the human heart. Sometimes these ideas seem to get their inspiration partially from the fact that they appear to have been missed by everyone else. Your heart's cry is, "Why doesn't someone see this?" or "Why doesn't anyone do something?" This is because God has put the solution that will make a difference into your heart and not in the heart of someone else.

It is your part to visualize and meditate on the vision God has given you and, by agreeing with God, it is brought to pass. Often we wait to take action on the vision until we become frustrated. I would highly suggest proceeding with some form of action, even if only in small incremental ways. This will help you avoid developing disappointment about the vision. It is not God's heart for you to become frustrated over the vision. In His timing, it is a pure joy to see the vision come to pass. Our problem is, most of the time, God's timing is much loooooooooooonger that we anticipated.

Typically, the first lie that comes against an inspirational thought or vision is that it is not from God. You may have these thoughts: you just made it up, it is something you want to do, or you are just saying it is God. I am going to explain to you how foolish these lies really are. You see, God gave you the vision, but it was something you already had in your heart. That is not making it up. God put it in your heart because He knew you would love to bring it to fruition. God knows what you like; He is your Creator. God's heart is for you to experience joy, and the most joy you can have is living in His plan for your life. God knows what you like to do better than you do.

The lie that God will force you into something that you do not want to do is an absolute misconception of how He operates.

How many of you have seen a father who loves baseball or other sports, but his son likes music or some other activity? If you see that same father pushing his son to play baseball, what do you think about him as a dad? You may think of him as a bad father and, in this area, he is because his motivation is self-centered. It is based on his desire and not the child's. God is not like this at all. 1 Corinthians 13:5 says that love, *"...does not seek its own."* God is love; therefore, He is never selfish. God is interested in what you are interested in because God is a good Dad! The idea, in a way, is yours, but God stirs creativity and passion to give you the motivation to accomplish the vision. This could be compared to the parent who is trying to get their musically gifted child to the best teachers and schools. Or the parent who sees the athletic skill of a child and spends time training them earlier than their peers. The important point is that the desire comes from the child's heart and not the parent's. A good parent may plant the idea as a seed, but the child must want to see it grow. God is a good Father. If you like baseball, He likes baseball. If you like model cars, He likes model cars. He is the perfect Father. He will plant the seed in idea form, but He will never push you into something that you are not supposed to do. You will not end up in a hut in Africa unless you love the hut, or at least, care so much about the people that the hut is irrelevant.

The lie that God will force you into something that you do not want to do is an absolute misconception of how God operates. He would first instill a love for the African people in you. Through that love, you would envision creative ideas to help them. The joy of His heart would be to see your vision come to pass for the people you both care about. So, even though the conditions might be difficult, you would be experiencing the joy of the Lord in that hut in Africa. You would have the joy of knowing that your destiny for being on the earth was being fulfilled. There is no greater satisfaction in this life.

Am I being deceived out of my destiny?

Why would God create six billion unique people, hoping they would accept His love, only to destroy their uniqueness to make them just like His Son?

Let's look at Galatians 2:20 to point out a deceptive trick the enemy has used with this verse. *"I have been crucified with Christ; it is no longer I who live, but Christ lives in me; and the life which I now live in the flesh I live by faith in the Son of God, who loved me and gave Himself for me."* It is easy to read this scripture from a religious works mindset and suppose you should have your personality destroyed so God will be able to do something good through you. If that is what it means, why would God create six billion unique people then hope they would accept His love, only to destroy their uniqueness to make them just like His Son? That does not make any sense at all! This is because it is a deception to alter the intended meaning of the verse. This verse is not about self-abasement. Some people who read this verse feel ashamed and think they need to destroy their personalities in order to be more like Jesus. I personally believe the perversion of this verse is what would be considered a "doctrine of devils" as spoken of in I Timothy 4:1.

This verse is not about changing your personality, but about who will be in charge now that you have made Jesus your Lord. Read it like this, **"I"** have been crucified with Christ; it is no longer **"I"** who live. This verse is saying your selfish motives and desires that are only in your own best interest, **"the I"** who was you, is now dead. The new you is submitted to your Lord Jesus's interests which extend way beyond your own selfish desires. That is what Jesus is referring to in Luke 9:23-24 when He says, *"If anyone desires to come after Me, let him deny himself, and take up his cross daily, and follow me.*

For whoever desires to save his life will lose it, but whoever loses his life for My sake will save it." Taking up your own cross is about voluntary submission to God's leadership, not self-abasement or the destruction of your personality. God wants you to be the best <u>you</u> that is possible. He does not wish to destroy His Own original work of art, you.

The best plan for your life is the plan in which the most qualified leader is in charge, and between you and God, that would be God.

Through the submission of your life to the Lordship of Jesus, God reveals to you who you are really meant to be. When you voluntarily give up the right to govern your own life, then God is able to lead you in the paths of righteousness for His name's sake that are spoken of in Psalms 23:3. God is a good Father. He doesn't want to kill you, He wants to get you in the best position to have an abundant life (John 10:10). That position is under His authority. The best plan for your life is the plan in which the most qualified leader is in charge and, between you and God that would be God.

I received a very similar revelation several years ago when I was asking God for an understanding of Matthew 11:28-30. *"Come to Me, all you who labor and are heavy laden, and I will give you rest. Take My yoke upon you and learn from Me, for I am gentle and lowly in heart, and you will find rest for your souls. For My yoke is easy and My burden is light."* I was confused about the phrase <u>burden is light</u> because the Christian life, at times, seems difficult. God said to me, <u>burden of command</u>. As soon as I heard this thought, I immediately understood what God meant.

The term burden of command is given to describe the weight of responsibility that a military commander feels over the lives of those under his command. The realization that people may live or die based on their decisions is very stressful, both mentally and emotionally. God was trying to clarify that His yoke is to be easy and His burden is to be light because we are no longer the ones who have the burden of command over our own lives. With Jesus as our Lord we are no longer calling the shots. We are, so to speak, just soldiers taking orders from our superior Officer. Once we relinquish the burden of command, our life should be much easier without the responsibility of its leadership. If you find yourself stressed and anxious then check to see if you may have taken back the responsibility of running your own life. Relinquish that responsibility back to the Lord Jesus and rest in His ability to lead. You are not meant to handle the burden of command of your own life. Jesus, alone, is the One capable of managing that responsibility. Your yoke is easy and your burden is light.

Jesus does not want to run your life because He is a dictatorial tyrant, but because you are not qualified to run it yourself. You are easily fooled by your own heart, not to mention the deceptions of others. Jeremiah 17:9-10 says, *"The heart is deceitful above all things, and desperately wicked; who can know it? I, the Lord, search the heart, I test the mind, even to give to every man according to his ways, according to the fruit of his doings."* Once you realize you have a good heavenly Father Who loves you and desires to see what He has placed in your heart come to pass, then, and only then, are you free to be yourself. In the freedom that comes with this accurate understanding of your relationship with God, imagination and creativity flourish.

There is only one part of this relationship which may feel negative: God's truthfulness. God is absolutely truthful. He is not willing to allow you to live in any form of deception. God's heart is freedom.

He will lovingly expose what could be called issues in your life, so that you can experience total freedom. It may feel negative when a vulnerable area is initially exposed, but as we experience more and more freedom, we can look forward to this process knowing the end result is more freedom.

Why do I feel like I am going nuts?

At times there can be an apparent hypocrisy in our Christian life. This is because as we are growing in our relationship with God, He is revealing issues in our heart. This may make us feel like we are hypocrites as more of our deceptions are being exposed. We may feel like we are going backwards compared to the freedom we see for our future. Satan will use these feelings of hypocrisy to harass you with lies like: you are a hypocrite; you have all this junk in your life and you call yourself a Christian. Other favorites of his can be: if people only knew who you really are, what would they think; you have been dealing with this stuff so long and you're no better; why don't you just quit and go back to the way you were, at least you won't be a hypocrite. Does any of this sound familiar? Ironically, it is during this time of the most spiritual progress that Satan is able to hinder our development through these deceptions.

The issues being brought up are evidence that God is active in your life.

Here is a key to identifying this deception. Who is the focus of these thoughts? Satan is a master at taking the focus off what God is doing and has <u>already done</u> in your life and putting it on your current performance. Don't go there with him. If this turns out to be about our performance then we all will fail. It is not about our performance, but Jesus's performance and His work is perfect. No matter how you feel, there is no hypocrisy in your life if you are submitted to God's leadership. It doesn't matter how much old junk you are working through emotionally. The issues being brought up are evidence that God is active in your life. If nothing is being brought up to yield to His Lordship, you might need to question if you are under God's leadership at all.

How do I walk into my destiny?

At some point God may stir a creative idea that grows in your heart. It does not have to pertain to a subject you would label as spiritual. Perhaps you want to play an instrument or make something by hand. The main thing is that you really care about it. There is glory on actions performed with passion from our heart. That is how God's glory is revealed in you. His glory is revealed because we have been liberated to be who we really are and, in that freedom, God's kingdom is manifested on this earth.

Christians who are focused on performance can be deceived by attempting to assess what would be the best thing for them to do based on some spiritual sliding scale of worth. They may never even consider that what they really want to do could be the best option. Remember, God is a good Dad; He likes what you like. In your unique passions is where His glory will be clearly seen. You are free and God is talking to you as you are being led by His Spirit. That is the <u>riches of the glory of His inheritance in the saints</u>. Saint Augustine summed this up rather succinctly when he said, "Love God and do whatever you please; for the soul trained in love to God will do nothing to offend the One who is Beloved." Doesn't that sound a lot easier than the spiritual burden of trying to figure out what you should be doing next?

Since the most important treasure in the world lies in the hearts of men and women, the most important assignment you will ever have is to influence their hearts.

The heart of who you were made to be rests in finding out how your uniqueness can best be utilized to serve your fellow man. Since the most important treasure in the world lies in the hearts of men and women, the most important assignment you will ever have is to influence their hearts. In the Christian world this is call ministry. What does it really mean to minister to the needs of other people? To serve someone as a minister in a very tangible way is to be the equivalent of a prospector. You are someone who, through the guidance of the Holy Spirit, is uncovering the precious jewels that lie hidden in who God created them to be. I referred earlier to Ephesians 1:18 which says the riches of the glory of God's inheritance is in the saints. The most priceless gems on earth are the deposits that God has made in the hearts of men and women. The difference between a prospector and a minister is that the minister knows the location of the treasure. All the true riches on this earth are in the people. One of the ways the riches are mined out of the people is through the developing of relationships. God loves the positive effects that happen when people relate with one another under the inspiration of His love.

One time I was giving a bid to perform service work for a local Jewish synagogue and God used that experience to teach me a lot about fellowship. I measured the actual meeting area and was amazed that it was extremely small for the size of the congregation. I could not understand its small size as the building itself was very large. Next, I proceeded to measure the dining hall which was one of the largest that I had ever seen. This congregation of Jewish believers had put their priority on the relationships within their fellowship. In the Christian church, for the most part, we have placed our priority on teaching. This really made me start to seriously wonder if this emphasis on relationship was more correct than the emphasis of the modern Christian church. After years of study, I now believe it is.

Some of the best things that will ever happen to you will occur when small groups of believers are just spending time together. When believers get together they are already in agreement as to Who is in charge of their lives and for that reason, when they gather together, there is spiritual power released. You don't have to be in a traditional church service to have a life changing experience. The church is the bride of Christ no matter where or when she is meeting.

How will you answer your call?

By comparing the responses of two people when God reveals their destiny, I think we can learn the best way to embrace God's plan for our future. The first person we will look at is Mary, the mother of Jesus. The account is in Luke 1:26-38. Mary, as a young virgin, is visited by an angel and told that she has been chosen to be the mother of God's Son. Mary questions the angel because she has never been with a man. This is a very legitimate question given the fact that a virgin birth had never occurred in all of human history. After the angelic explanation, we read her response in verse 38, *"Behold the maidservant of the Lord! Let it be to me according to your word."* This is total submission to something that is humanly impossible. There is such trust in this young woman toward God; it is absolutely beautiful to me. She is basically saying that if you said it, then that is how it will be. I love her heart. The only way to receive all that God has for your future is by <u>trusting in Him to bring it to pass</u> even when you cannot see any way it is possible. Especially, if you cannot see a way.

The next person we will look at is Moses. At this stage of his life Moses is eighty years old, living on the backside of a desert after having fled Egypt at the age of forty to avoid imprisonment for murder. The story is recorded in Exodus Chapters 3 and 4. God reveals to Moses that He is now ready to free the Hebrew people from their captivity in Egypt, and He is going to send Moses to deliver them. At this time Moses begins a long list of reasons why he (Moses) is not the one: 3:11, I am not that important; 3:14, they will not know who You are; 4:1, they will not believe You spoke to me; and 4:10, I do not speak well. Finally Moses ends with 4:13, *"O my Lord, please send by the hand of whomever else You may send."*

Moses, simply put, did not want to fulfill what God was proclaiming as his destiny. But, didn't I tell you that God will not force you to do something you do not want to do? The fact is, Moses has wanted this his entire life. His fugitive status was brought about by the murder of an Egyptian slave master who was abusing a Hebrew slave. Moses had known most of his life that freeing his people was his destiny, but now at eighty years old, he does not have enough faith <u>in his own abilities</u> to bring it to pass. Moses had lost all hope that his destiny would be fulfilled. Even with God revealing it Himself in a supernatural way, Moses still does not believe.

God wants to implant a vision in your heart for your future, but most of us immediately think that we have the key role in "bringing it to pass".

I want to highlight the difference between Mary's and Moses's responses to unlock a key to your future. Mary trusted in God to do something impossible while Moses did not believe God because he could not see how it was possible for him (Moses) to do it. Many of us make the key mistake Moses made. We think that bringing our future to pass has more to do with our abilities than it does God's abilities. Having not been with a man, Mary knew she was not able to be a virgin mother. At eighty, Moses was assessing whether he had what it took to pull off the mission God was giving him. God wants to implant a vision in your heart for your future, but most of us immediately think that we have the key role in bringing it to pass. That is not our role in the vision. <u>Our role, like Mary's, is simply to believe God who gave the vision</u>. When we argue with God about the vision, what we are really saying is: I cannot accomplish it in my own strength. While the truth of the matter is, it is not about our strength, but God's strength.

Who is responsible for bringing my destiny to pass?

Let me make this very clear. God is not asking you to bring your destiny to pass. He can do it by Himself; after all, He is God! He is challenging you to participate with Him in something you both mutually care about. Can you even imagine what Moses's heart was feeling as He led the Hebrews out of Egypt? To lead an entire nation of your own people to freedom in a single day must have been one of the greatest feelings a man has ever felt on this earth. Psalms 37:4 says, *"Delight yourself also in the Lord, and He shall give you the desires of your heart."* God was giving Moses his heart's desire, even after Moses had given up on the vision himself. To me that is one of the greatest testimonies about the faithfulness of God. This is proof that God desires for you to fulfill your destiny even more than you do.

But, what is our role in our destiny? Our role is the same as Mary's role: to believe the vision and receive the <u>seed</u> of destiny; to cherish and nurture this gift of God. It is our role to be grateful that God allows us to participate in His Divine eternal plans. The reality is that God can reveal Himself to the world in a single moment, but like Moses, He desires that we participate with Him in the joy of delivering others. Remember the first point I ever spoke about: God is relational and always will be. You are in His relationship circle because you are united with Jesus through the marriage contract. God really desires for us to have an active part in His plans and purposes, but that does not mean that He is incapable of handling it Himself.

The joy God experiences when you participate in His dreams, by dreaming with Him, is what He gets excited about. During our engagement period, God wants us to develop our heart to care about what He cares about. This is so that when we stand on the day of the wedding, we are already one at heart. You were left on earth to develop a deeper intimacy with God by caring about who He cares about - people.

There are enemies, both external and internal, who will try to hinder our development in the selfless pursuit of caring for others. Alongside our external enemy, the devil, there is the internal enemy of our own selfishness. We can be so caught up in ourselves that we neglect building our relationship with God. Our work, according to John 6:29, is to believe in the One God sent. Believing God keeps the vision in play so that it can come to pass. However, our own self-centeredness undermines our ability to believe.

If we stop and consider that God could just as easily use a jackass, then we will develop the proper heart of gratitude for His allowing our participation in His plans.

God could have picked a lizard to deliver the children of Israel out of slavery. I can show you in Numbers 22:25-30 where God allowed a talking donkey to save a man's life. We need to realize that, when ministering to others, we are a channel of communication to those He loves. If we stop and consider that God could just as easily use a jackass, then we will develop the proper heart of gratitude for His allowing our participation in His plans. Remember, it is not the method that God cares about, but the motive. His motive is love for people and He loves for people to be free. Moses was just a method to achieve that end, but it was the joy of God's heart that His friend Moses shared His vision. God loved Moses too much to leave him out of this mission. Even if He had to take him along kicking and screaming like a little child who does not know what is best for him.

The knowledge of how much God cares was the driving factor in Jesus's mission to rescue His bride. Isaiah 53:11 says, "...*By His knowledge My righteous Servant shall justify many, for He shall bear their iniquities.*" Jesus knew something that caused Him to bear the sins of mankind on the cross. This cannot be referring to Christ's knowledge of astrophysics or biochemistry. It is by the knowledge of His Father's heart that Jesus was able to endure the cross. Jesus shared God's love for mankind before we were ever created. He decided to participate in that love as the centerpiece of its demonstration. All Three Persons of the Trinity have always loved you and have always been in agreement about your worth before you were ever created. *"Just as He chose us in Him before the foundation of the world, that we should be holy and without blame before Him in love" (Ephesians 1:4).*

How does God get glory from my life?

If God shows you a future that is big and outlandish in proportion to where you are now; believe it. There is freedom in knowing you could not possibly achieve it if you tried. After years of anxiety, I cannot fully explain how freeing it was to realize that it does not all depend on me. This is a lighter yoke, indeed. In this freedom your creativity will soar because this is where you discover your individuality. If God shows you a picture of your future, daydream about it. God's desire is that you will imagine and even co-create with Him.

Eternal impact can only be achieved by those under God's Leadership.

Steve Jobs, the deceased co-founder of Apple Inc., daydreamed and drew pictures of the iPad long before the technology existed to make it.^ It can be said that men and women who have accomplished great things on this earth have tapped into a source bigger than themselves for their inspiration. God can inspire anyone to make a positive difference, but a lasting, eternal impact can only be achieved by those under His leadership.

What Jesus had imparted to His disciples was more than could be explained by their human abilities. After the disciples, Peter and John, had testified before the High Council of the Jews, this was the Council's observation, *"Now when they saw the boldness of Peter and John, and perceived that they were uneducated and untrained men, they marveled. And they realized that they had been with Jesus" (Acts 4:13).* What the disciples were doing was above their own capabilities. Once people realize you are neither smart nor talented enough to accomplish what you are doing, God gets the glory. This is right where you want to be and is the highest compliment that anyone can give you.

The same thing happened to the Jewish exiles who returned to Jerusalem and rebuilt the city walls in 52 days. This feat was not humanly possible and is recorded in the book of Nehemiah. God always gets honored at these times because, if it cannot be attributed to human ability, God is the only logical conclusion to the outcome. We can be sure God gets the maximum glory from our lives by not taking the lead ourselves. We are about to take an extended look at the obstructions which attempt to prevent our destiny from coming to pass, and what we can do to fight against them.

[A]Steve Jobs Copyright © 2011 by Walter Isaacson, Publisher Simon & Shuster

Section 2

Knowing How Your Heart Works

Chapter 7

How Do I Understand My Own heart?

What is the heart?

The best definition that I can give for the word <u>heart</u> is: core beliefs. The Hebrew word mainly used for <u>heart</u> in the Old Testament means: the feelings, the will and even intellect, and conveys the center. The New Testament Greek word mainly used for <u>heart</u> means: the thoughts or feelings, (mind) and conveys the middle. Can the heart referred to in the Bible only mean the feelings? I believe the answer lies in where those feelings originate: your core beliefs. You cannot have genuine feelings about anything unless they originate from your core beliefs on the subject. This explains perfectly the level of passion that we see on both sides of the Pro-Life/Pro-Choice debate. Both sides believe their position on a level that is much deeper than head knowledge alone.

What moves you to anger? What stirs compassion in you? What moves you to take action? When we say two people are of the same mind (their core beliefs), then they are in absolute agreement with what they believe on a heart level. Since the heart also means the middle or center of anything, what you believe to be true at the center of your beliefs is your heart on the subject. These are the beliefs you will act upon concerning that subject. It is one thing to mentally comprehend the right to vote, but your voting record displays your heart (core beliefs) on the subject of voting. On a more emotional note; it is one thing to say you love someone, but do you do what is in their best interest over and above your own interest? That is your actual core belief (heart) which testifies of your love for them. Jesus loves you. He thought of your interest over and above His own (Philippians 2:5-11).

Do I think in my heart?

"Wait a minute. I don't think in my heart!"

I was driving down the road one day contemplating the meaning of a Bible verse. It was the first part of Proverbs 23:7 which says, *"For as He thinks in his heart, so is he..."*. I had thought about this verse often, but had overlooked a clue to understanding its deeper meaning. That particular day I had this simple thought, **"Wait a minute. I don't think in my heart!"** The chain of events that followed that one thought resulted in a simple, yet profound, understanding of the human heart. God has led me to use this understanding to release many people from a life of disillusionment, and to chart a course to where they are truly meant to live. I thank God for the simplicity of what I am about to share with you. I pray it will help you as it has helped others. I will be referring often to **Diagram B**, "Battle for Your Heart".

You cannot believe something unless you have thought it first.

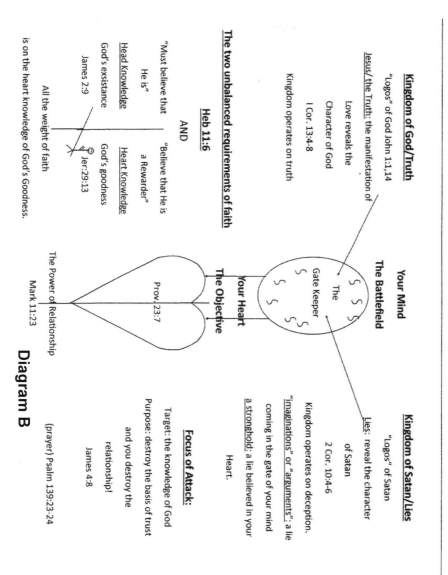

Diagram B

How did this simple revelation, <u>I don't think in my heart,</u> open my understanding of the human condition? When I began to study the word <u>thinks</u> in the Hebrew language, I found it to be very descriptive. It means: gatekeeper. Therefore, the verse is literally saying as a man keeps the gate of his heart so is he. A gate is used to let something in or keep something out. This is why we use the term gateway for a point of entry. What then is the gateway of the heart? Without a doubt, it has to be the mind. In **Diagram B** I have drawn the mind as the entry point into the heart. This is because you cannot believe something unless you have thought it first.

The mind is the processor of all your thoughts, but the heart is the hard drive of the system. I want us to look at an important warning that God gives about the heart in Proverbs 4:23, *"Guard your heart with all diligence; for out of it spring the issues of life."* Some Bible translations use the word <u>keep</u> instead of <u>guard</u>, but it still has the same meaning which is: to protect or guard. Notice, it is not saying to guard your mind. If you have a meandering mind, you could have thought about five different things in the last few minutes. I have even called people and, while the phone is ringing, forgotten who I called because I was thinking of something else. The mind is just the processor; it doesn't matter how much information goes through it. What is significant is what gets stored onto the hard drive of our heart . But, what are we supposed to be guarding our hearts from? The answer is just one thing: LIES!

How do lies get in my heart?

All of your actions proceed from what you believe to be true in your heart, whether it is actually true or not.

Lies are planted in our heart. A thought, whether true or false, comes into our mind; we can generate it or it can come from another source. When a thought comes in, we can either accept it as truth or reject it as a lie. If we accept a thought, then it proceeds to be stored into our heart and becomes part of our belief system. This belief system is how you interpret and filter your world. You operate according to what you believe to be true in your heart and all of your actions proceed from that belief whether it is actually true or not. This is why God warns us in Proverbs 4:23 to guard our heart.

Since the heart will believe whatever it has accepted; as a guide for truth, it cannot be trusted. God warns us about this in Jeremiah 17:9-10, *"The heart is deceitful above all things, and desperately wicked; who can know it? I, the Lord, search the heart, I test the mind, even to give every man according to his ways, according to the fruit of his doings."* The word <u>deceitful</u> here means: tracked. This is like a well-worn path which got that way by constant use. By exposing these evil, yet familiar paths I am giving you the opportunity to choose another way and to blaze a new path bathed in the light of truth. The verse says that God gives to you according to your ways. The word <u>ways</u> means: trodden paths or course of life. By choosing to live a life apart from the deceptive tricks of your own heart, you are blazing a trail which will lead you to that place where you are able to receive the maximum blessing of God in your life.

By having you bring up an old memory, I will demonstrate how lies lodge in your heart as strongholds. I would like you to recall an instance when you were very young; when you were in elementary/middle school, or even younger. Think of a time when something very negative was said to you. Think of a parent, friend, coach, or teacher as a reference to jog your memory. When I ask most people to recall a particular instance, many recall every detail about the event.

They remember the room, the color of the walls, where they were standing, and the body position of the other person. This is equally true of people who normally don't have good memories. How is this possible? When you hear words like, "you'll never amount to anything" or "you're ugly", these can go quickly through the mind. They can be internally processed as truth, which is believed in the heart as fact. When you are young and the person was someone you loved or respected, the new belief will anchor in your heart almost immediately. This is the reason for the accurate recall: that moment was so traumatic it went straight into your heart. It was like getting kicked in the chest and, emotionally, you were.

Let's read what Jesus said in John 8:31-32 and then I have a question, *"If you abide in My word, you are My disciples indeed and you shall know the truth, and the truth shall make you free."* Does the truth set you free? Not exactly. <u>Knowing the truth</u> is what makes you free. Just because someone is aware of the truth of Who God is doesn't make them free. Satan does not doubt Who God is, yet is he free? Knowing the truth is more than just a mental ascent to the facts. James 2:19 says, *"You believe there is one God. You do well. Even the demons believe – and tremble!"* Jesus said in John 14:6, *"I am the way, the truth, and the life. No one comes to the Father except through Me."* Since the truth is a <u>Person</u>, we could not say we <u>know</u> Him if we are only aware that He exists.

Acknowledging the truth will not make you free, but continuing in a relationship with the Truth is the only way to truly know Him and be set free.

The Truth is Jesus. The truth is knowing what God is really like through the love He showed us in Jesus. You come to know the Truth by continuing to abide under the direction and leadership of God. Satan and his demons cannot know God relationally, because they will not submit to His Lordship in their lives. Acknowledging the truth will not make you free, but continuing in a relationship with the Truth is the only way to truly know Him and be set free.

What is the difference between arguments and strongholds?

In 2 Corinthians 10:3-6 we can get a clearer understanding of how these lies come to us. *"For though we walk in the flesh, we do not war according to the flesh. For the weapons of our warfare are not carnal but mighty in God for pulling down strongholds, casting down arguments and every high thing that exalts itself against the knowledge of God, bringing every thought into captivity to the obedience of Christ."* It clearly says that the war we are in is not physical, but spiritual. I am going to give you some simple definitions that will clarify some of the words used in this passage. For years I heard teachings on these verses, but they were always too complicated or vague to be useful.

The simple definition of a stronghold is: a believed lie. The simple definition of an argument is: a lie. Lies are rebellious ideas that come against the truth. That is why they are called arguments; they are arguing against the truth. A stronghold is a lie that made it into your heart. The belief in the lie has strengthened the lie and made it a stronghold. If I were to draw a wall in your heart it would represent what took place; the lie was believed by you as truth. This has become a wall of deception against the actual truth. The more lies someone has believed, the more walled off their heart is to the truth. It is also the degree to which they walk in self-deception.

What do I do when my good is bad?

As surprising as this may sound, these strongholds do not always manifest themselves in completely negative symptoms. However, they always have a negative effect on the person who has believed them. Someone who has heard a parent tell them they will never amount to anything, and believed that lie, could grow up never trying to accomplish anything with their life. However, the same person could respond with an "I'll show them" attitude. There are billionaires who have never enjoyed their wealth because of a believed lie driving them to prove their worth. No matter what your response is to the belief, if the stronghold is driving your life, you are not in a positive position. It may look good to the world that you are driven or have a great work ethic, but the truth is that you are living in a stronghold of deception. No matter how attractive the side effects, the lie is still in charge.

Philippians 4:6-7 says, *"Be anxious for nothing, but in everything by prayer and supplication, with thanksgiving, let your requests be made known to God; and the peace of God, which surpasses all understanding, will guard your hearts and minds through Christ Jesus."* In God's kingdom there is peace when you ask for it and are willing to let go of the lies. If there is an anxiousness that runs your life or if you catch yourself driven to finish this book, please stop, put it down, and be vulnerable before God. These obsessive lies make everything into a punch list that you must complete, but you already know that the list never ends. God is right here and He loves you even if you never do another thing. You are completely accepted in Jesus, His Son. Your works do not gain you the acceptance of your Father God because you are already accepted. There are no strings attached. God loves you, period.

I declare the power of conditional acceptance to be broken in your life by the power of the work of Jesus. The hammer of the word of God has hit this stronghold in your heart and it shall never be repaired. I magnify the last words of Jesus, so they will resonate in your spirit, "It is finished". He has overcome your deception and He, Who is the Truth of God, shall prevail in your life. Repeat these words with me: I refuse to be accepted for what I do; I am valuable; I am worth the life of Jesus Christ; God loves me and there is nothing that I can do about it; I am free. If your heart is being changed at this moment it is because Satan sowed the lie of conditional acceptance in your heart. I would encourage you go to youtube.com and type in "The Anthem (Full Song) Planetshakers". This song declares that you are freed only through the work of Jesus and not anything you can do personally.

How shallow is my enemy?

Satan's kingdom only exists to bring lies against the truth.

There are two kingdoms listed on **Diagram B**. The Kingdom of God or Kingdom of Truth is made up of everything that is Truth. It represents the self-sacrificial loving heart of God. It is best displayed in Jesus who is called the Word of God (John 1:1,14). In the Greek the word in that passage is logos and it means: the thing said including the intent behind it. The base of the same word used to describe Jesus as the logos of God is also used for the word arguments in 2 Corinthians 10:5. The kingdom of Satan or kingdom of lies represents Satan's heart which is full of deceit. It manifests itself as these arguments, or the logos of Satan. The Kingdom of Truth has its depth in self-sacrificial love, while the kingdom of lies exists only to lie against God's Kingdom of Truth.

What scripture best describes the motive of the kingdom of lies compared to the Kingdom of Truth? I believe it would be hard to beat John 10:10, *"The thief does not come except to steal, and to kill, and to destroy. I [Jesus] have come that they might have life, and that they might have it more abundantly."* The characteristics of the kingdom of lies are all similar in nature. They are: to take away possession (steal), to take away life (kill), and to take away usefulness (destroy). Every action of this kingdom comes out of a heart motive of taking.

The shallowness of Satan's kingdom can best be shown by looking at it contrasted with God's Kingdom. The characteristic of the Kingdom of Truth is to give life, so that those who receive it could grow and flourish abundantly. The heart motive of God's kingdom is giving. One kingdom is selfless; the other selfish. The attribute of God that sticks out most in my mind is that God does not seek His own. This means He is never looking out for His own interest, ever. God is only thinking about what He <u>can do for you</u>; never what He <u>can get out of you</u>. One kingdom is take, take, take and the other is give, give, give (John 10:10). That is about as drastic a contrast as one could imagine. Because of this drastic difference a simple shortcut to discern whether a thought is a truth or a lie is to ask this question: "Will this thought give something to me or will this thought take something away from me?"

I want to make it clear that the complete depth of Satan's kingdom only exists to bring lies against the truth. I want you to see how shallow your enemy is. His only weapon is deception. If you do not receive a lie, his kingdom of lies can have no power over you. Part of Satan's masterful deception is to make people believe he is more powerful than he is, but should you ever believe a deceiver that tells you he is powerful?

This makes me think of the blowfish. If the blowfish was already large, then it would not need to blow up in size to make you think that it is. Likewise, if Satan were already powerful, he would not need to make you think he is. Jesus spoke about Satan's deceptive character to some religious leaders who had embraced his same ways. *"You are of your father the devil, and the desires of your father you want to do. He was a murderer from the beginning, and does not stand in the truth, because there is no truth in him. When he speaks a lie, he speaks from his own resources, for he is a liar and the father of it"* (John 8:44). God is the Father of Jesus, Who men have spoken about for thousands of years without exhausting His attributes. Satan is the father of lies, and that is the full extent of what can be said about the offspring he reproduces.

Second Corinthians 10:5 says we are to cast down arguments. Some translations use the word imaginations instead of arguments. This is not referring to creative imagination, but is referring to vain or lofty imagined ideas against the truth. The word for <u>casting</u> in the Greek means: to bring down, to demolish or destroy. Therefore, the process to destroy a lie would look like this. If you heard the thought or comment, "You're an idiot!" you would simply refuse it by saying or merely thinking, "No, I am not." This thought or comment will carry no influence over you as long as you disagree and cast it out of your mind. That is why the term casting is used. It is just like casting aside something unwanted. If you initially reject a lie at the mind level, allowing it to go no further, then it is a very simple process.

How do I fight in the battlefield of my mind?

"Going around the mountain again" is easily explained. Our stronghold (believed lie) was not completely destroyed.

What does 2 Corinthians 10:4 say we are to do with strongholds (believed lies)? We are to pull them down. The word used for pull here in the Greek means: demolition, extinction, or complete destruction. This is explaining that a lie, at the mind level, can be cast aside, but a believed lie (a stronghold) in our heart must be completely destroyed. To remove a stronghold the rejection must be a more purposeful process because the lie has become entrenched in our belief system. All the elements of the lie must be continuously resisted until they are obliterated. We must firmly commit at the heart level to have absolutely no agreement with any part of the previous lie (our dying stronghold).

You may have had the experience, as a Christian, that an old problem or an aggravating belief just keeps resurfacing. We call this, "going around the mountain again". The reason for this is easily explained. Our stronghold (believed lie) was not completely destroyed. Even after counseling or major life changes it can still be there. This is because we still agree with some part of the lie in our heart. *"As he thinks in his heart, so is he" (Proverbs 23:7)*. You will always act out of the beliefs in your heart. There is no way to permanently make effective change in your behavior without changing your heart. This is good news because, by exposing the lie and refusing it when it tries to return, we can all be completely free.

This subject is not an attempt to increase our introspection. This is not about so-called navel gazing. We are only taking an inner look for two reasons: to be free and to not be deceived again. There is a lot of power in being aware of your enemy's tactics. 2 Corinthians 2:11 says, *"Lest Satan should take advantage of us; for we are not ignorant of his devices."* If you are hearing the lie that you are being too introspective then please, trust me and fight through it. This book is only using the word of God for counsel. We will be discovering some very useful strategies from God's word to help us fight in this war and win.

I would like to give you a personal example of how I used the revelation of my enemy's strategies to avoid deception. When I am teaching this material to a group of people, before class starts I will draw one of these diagrams on the board. I am usually by myself, but there may be one or two people in the back of the room working on sound. The last time I drew a diagram these were the actual thoughts that I heard in my head: "You have taught this before, it is not that important"; "This is stupid, you are not in sync with the people tonight"; "You're not feeling that great right now, this is dumb." Now I had a choice to believe any or all of those lies. Do you know what I did? I laughed to myself and replied: "You're saying nothing new. Thanks for letting me know I am on track." When you are thanking the devil because his strategy has alerted you to your effectiveness that is a position of strength. We can all walk in this strength when we are aware of his schemes, and are unwilling to allow ourselves to be deceived by the previously wounded areas in our hearts. Removing the strongholds eliminates the most difficult part of spiritual warfare. <u>If you no longer have strongholds, your warfare is reduced to the casting aside of lies, and this is a much simpler process.</u>

What does Satan's focus of attack reveal?

If you are in a war and your enemy attacks one area over and over again, what does that tell you?

It is crucial that we recognize a point made in 2 Corinthians 10. In verse five we see that the target of these evil forces is the knowledge of God. The arguments, the strongholds, and every high thing have one single target: the knowledge of God. If you are in a war and your enemy attacks one area over and over again, what does it tell you? It tells you that this particular area is the key to winning the war. Strategically, it is either the most important area or the area of greatest vulnerability. The correct understanding of God is the most important area and our willingness to doubt His character is our area of greatest vulnerability.

I explained earlier that you are the object of God's affection; you were created to be the bride of Christ. Many of you have been Christians for years and have never heard these two statements, yet they are true. You have not heard them because you have an enemy who opposes one area above all others: the knowledge of what God is really like. Satan, at all costs, does not want you to know the character of God. Knowing the truth of how much God loves you is Satan's biggest fear because your courage comes from this knowledge. *"There is no fear in love; but perfect love casts out fear, because fear involves torment. But he who fears has not been made perfect in love"* (I John 4:18). If you understand <u>on a heart level</u> how much God loves you, then Satan's lies lose their power. You may have heard the words in your mind, but when you believe it <u>in your heart</u> is when they lose their power.

Chapter 8

Who Are the Enemies of My Freedom?

What are some examples of common lies?

I would like to give you an example of a simple lie we have all heard: "You are stupid." If you are a relatively intelligent person, with no background of hearing that lie, you can cast it aside quickly. If you heard that lie in the past and it was stored in your heart, you will react differently. If a parent or teacher said that to you at an early age, when you hear it again, you weigh it against your old memories. If the present lie confirms the old lie, the old stronghold (believed lie) is strengthened further. Someone can be brilliant, but not able to pass an exam because their heart tells them they are stupid. When a stronghold is in the heart it has to be acknowledged, resisted, and then replaced with the truth.

Be ready for a fight because a challenge will come quickly, giving you opportunity to agree with the old lie. For instance, you might lose your keys and you may hear thoughts like: "I am so stupid"; "I don't know a single person who loses their keys more than I do." Satan does not want to lose the ground of the stronghold because previously it was his occupied territory. You had previously given Satan a right to be in this area of your heart through your agreement with his lie. Now you have kicked him out and he wants back in. Notice this lie is you talking to yourself in agreement with the lie. Most of the time it sounds like we are the only ones involved in the lie; this is part of the deception.

When your value comes from outside of yourself, the attacks against you have no significance.

Many of the lies are ultimately about your identity, where you find your worth. If your worth is based on how much God loves you, then the lie that you are stupid cannot affect your identity. The truth is that you could be as dumb as a brick and be fine with it. Ultimate freedom is to be free from having your value tied to your performance. When your value comes from outside of yourself, the attacks against you have no significance. Jesus was completely free from a performance based identity. Jesus's identity was first tested when Satan came to Him in the wilderness. He tempted Jesus to prove His identity as the Son of God by turning the stones into bread and throwing Himself off a cliff (Luke 4: 1-13). It is imperative that we familiarize ourselves with this temptation. We are who God says we are: beloved sons and daughters. Satan will be tempting us to prove who we are through our performance.

Satan used the taunting of the Roman guards before Jesus's crucifixion to test Him once again on His identity. *"Now the men who held Jesus mocked Him and beat Him. And having blindfolded*

Him they struck Him on the face and asked Him, saying, Prophesy! Who is the one who struck You?" (Luke 22:63-64). If Jesus's identity was in His own abilities then He would have displayed them. Jesus is Commander of the armies of heaven, yet His identity was not in His own ability. Jesus's identity was in His Father's love for Him. *"… This is My beloved Son, in whom I am well pleased" (Mathew 3:17).*

If Satan's attacks are solely against knowing God, what does the lie that you are stupid have to do with knowing God? Personal insults are attacks to keep you from fulfilling your God given potential. If you believe that you are stupid, lazy, ugly, or any other personal insult, you will devalue yourself. The more your personal value is lowered, through believed lies, the more difficult it is for you to comprehend that God could possibly love someone like you. These strongholds make it harder to comprehend how much God loves you; therefore, they are actually directed at the same target, just from a different angle. The outcome of a devalued self-worth is a crippled ability to believe God's love and act on the plan He has for your future.

If you are not important, then why are you hearing "Kill yourself"? If you really don't matter at all, why are you hearing anything at all?

Another lie that has probably gone through your mind is that you are not worth anything; it would be better if you were dead. Most of us have heard that lie, but some of you have struggled with casting it aside more than others. This lie, of course, is trying to get you to kill yourself, but I would like to make a very strong point about any lie associated with suicide. This is the problem I have with the lie of suicide: if you are not important, why are you hearing kill yourself? If you really don't matter, why are you hearing anything at all? You should be hearing nothing, because you don't matter. The fact that you hear kill yourself is evidence that you are important! If you are being harassed by thoughts of suicide, then the lies themselves are overwhelming evidence that you are vitally important. In this spiritual war Satan does not waste his time on non-valuable targets. You are a target precisely because you are valuable. The lies against you validate your worth.

Why is my freedom so important?

Why is your freedom so important? God wants to see you reach the full potential of everything that He created you to be. However, there is another positive byproduct of freedom. Free people cannot tolerate seeing anyone else in bondage. This is a natural consequence of our personal freedom. A good example would be The United States of America which often involves herself with the internal affairs of other nations. I believe the root cause of this policy is much deeper than politics alone. Because we are a free nation, deep down, we just cannot tolerate the oppression of others. When a dictator or regime is oppressing a people group, even within a sovereign nation, we find this almost unbearable. We have been free so long that the core principle of freedom is in our hearts.

A stronghold in your own heart can stop the freedom of all those others whom you would have liberated had you been free yourself.

Free people set people free. The opposition to the removal of strongholds in our own heart has more ramifications than our own personal freedom. A stronghold in your own heart can stop the freedom of others you would have liberated had you been free yourself. Satan is terrified of free people because they endanger his kingdom by infecting others and reproducing freedom. The day that David killed Goliath, the entire Philistine army was also killed. David's freedom inspired the Hebrew army to act so fearlessly they destroyed the enemy's entire army.

In order to stop us from achieving this level of freedom, many of the lies we hear are individually crafted toward our personal history in the hope that they might find some past agreement. Satan is looking for weak spots, and will use any moments of previous vulnerability to establish a stronghold. You will be attacked where you are weak, so if you are already aware of these weak areas, the lies will not have the advantage of surprise. For example, a person may have had a bad experience in a relationship where the other party was hypocritical. They may have claimed to be one way, but were discovered to be something totally different. Satan will come with the lie that all men, or all women, are hypocrites. Since you have been wounded in this way, the last thing you desire is the possible pain another relationship could cause. Satan will target this wounded area hoping for agreement. He knows you will be prone to accept any lie to avoid the vulnerability of another relationship. Logically, you know that not every man or woman on earth is hypocritical, but because of your recent pain you are thinking emotionally not logically. If you accept this lie your agreement can develop into a root of bitterness toward the opposite sex. So, how will you be able to marry? Some people never do! Worse still, they never know God intimately because of that bitterness. This is a good example of kicking someone when they are down. Satan is the master of this technique.

Satan is the father of lies, but unless someone agrees with the lie, it has no power at all.

We are dealing with an enemy who is completely wicked. Satan will lie to a parent to get them to believe it is acceptable to sexually molest their child so that he might destroy the child's future. We are not dealing with a law-abiding enemy. There is nothing good in him at all. He wants you destroyed as quickly as possible, but deception is the only weapon in his arsenal. Someone has to agree with a lie in order for Satan's agenda to go forward. It is estimated that about twenty percent of people have experienced sexual abuse. The person who abused you is not innocent of their actions, but they are not the ultimate cause of your abuse. 2 Corinthians 10:3 says, *"For though we walk in the flesh, we do not war according to the flesh."* People are not the enemy. At any time they could repent and walk out of their deceptions, but they had to be in agreement with the lie in order to justify their abuse. Satan is the father of lies, but unless someone agrees with the lie, it has no power at all.

As you become stronger in spiritual warfare it becomes easier to separate the person who has abused you from the spiritual evil behind their actions. This is not a "letting them off the hook" sort of forgiveness, but an accurate understanding of the evil you have been and are still fighting against. We do not wrestle against flesh and blood. True forgiveness comes from an enlightened understanding of how your incredible worth has made you a target. To forgive those who agreed with Satan in your abuse is not to condone their actions, but to rise above letting what was done to you have an influence on your future. Continue to ask God for clearer discernment of the evil behind your abuse. He will give you the accurate understanding that you will need to extend the forgiveness necessary to walk in total freedom. No memory of prior abuse can further harm you as you understand how to reject the lies concerning the pain. You will most likely have a lie telling you the effects of your abuse will never end, but by now you know where the lie is coming from.

How does hypocrisy form in us?

Turn back to Proverbs 23:6-7, our original passage, for further insight into this battle we are engaged in. So far, we have only looked at part of the passage. *"Do not eat the bread of a miser, nor desire his delicacies; for as he thinks in his heart so is he. Eat and drink! He says to you, but his heart is not with you."* I have never heard anyone discuss the miser before. The focus had always been on "as he thinks in his heart". Therefore, what is the significance of the miser?

In this analogy the miser, who is a wealthy man, invites you over for dinner. However, he really does not want you eating his food, after all, he's a miser. The passage is describing to you the way he is thinking in his heart while, at the same time, he is speaking the opposite. He is telling you one thing, but thinking another; he is acting generous when, in actuality, he is stingy. In his heart, he has a stronghold of greed, selfishness, or pride. He might feel that you do not deserve the food he has worked so hard for, yet feel obligated to invite you. We are not completely sure of his motives.

If our hearts and minds are not in agreement we are hypocritical within our own selves.

The real problem here is one of hypocrisy. With his mouth or out of his mind he invited you for dinner, but in his heart there is something decidedly different. This passage is addressing the division that can exist inside all of us. The miser is speaking from his mind, but regretting his invitation in his heart. What is imperative is that we see that all of us are capable of doing the very same thing, if we do not get these strongholds out of our hearts. We can say one thing, but do we believe and act on another? In other words, is there agreement between our heart and our mind? James 1:8 speaks about a double-minded man who is unstable in all his ways. If our hearts and minds are not in agreement then we are hypocritical within our own selves. Since we are only one person, and cannot agree within ourselves, how are we going to function in our other relationships?

How can we see this in everyday relationships? If someone tells you that they love you, how can you know for sure? Where did it come from, their heart or their head? If they said I love you out of their mouth, it had to first go through their mind. But, how do you know what is in their heart? The answer is: by what they do over time. Our continued actions originate from within our hearts. If someone were to tell you that they love you, but when you go out on a date they pick the movie without asking your preference, that is their heart. If they do not ask you about your day or show interest in listening to you, then that is their heart. What people do over time tells you what is in their hearts. They can only consciously fake it for a short period of time. Just wait and you will have your answer. One of the most popular pop songs of all time is called "True Colors" and speaks about our hearts desire to see and be seen as we really are. I believe its popularity is based on a deep longing of the human heart.

> I'll see your true colors shining through
> I see your true colors, and that's why I love you
> So don't be afraid to let them show
> Your true colors, Your true colors
> Are beautiful like a rainbow
>
> - Cyndi Lauper

The core issue we are trying to eradicate in our personality is this hypocrisy. Whether we realize this or not, the opposite of hypocrisy is integrity. The word integrity has almost lost its true meaning. <u>Integrity</u> means: to be the same throughout. For instance, if I wanted to carve a statue out of marble, I would want the piece of marble to be of the utmost integrity. In other words, I want it to be 100 percent marble of the same quality throughout the entire piece of stone. Any flaws or imperfections in the stone could jeopardize the outcome of the finished statue.

When your heart and mind are in full agreement within yourself and with the Spirit of God, your life has integrity. With this integrity comes spiritual authority. When speaking directly from my heart to an audience, there are times when I am aware that I am in perfect agreement with God's heart. In those moments, there is a certain weightiness about what is being said. It is holy, as if God Himself where speaking. In those times God may give me analogies to explain His love that I have never thought of before, or He will connect Bible passages that I never knew were related. It is hard to explain what a joy it is to be a clear channel allowing the love of God to flow through me, impacting the people He so lovingly cares about.

How do we get this integrity? How do we get our hearts and minds in total agreement? Let me answer these important questions with a simpler question? How can you trust someone that you do not know? The simple answer is that you cannot. We as Christians try to work at trusting God while, often at the same time, we are not really getting to know God on a personal level. Have you ever experienced a feeling of guilt because you did not have enough faith for something to happen, while you knew in your heart that you should? I personally have felt this way many times. This used to trouble me greatly. I would beat myself up with thoughts like: how can I not believe God for this or what is my problem? The answer is simple. This is not a faith problem, this is a trust problem. How can I trust God when I really don't know Him? This is the real problem.

What is the difference in faith and trust?

Trust is based on the relationship, not your effort to believe (have faith) in the relationship.

How do you have more trust in someone? You cannot work up trust; you either have it or you don't. Trust is based on the relationship, not your effort to believe (have faith) in the relationship. You will trust God more as you get to know Him better, and you can only know Him better by spending more time in relationship. Great faith is accomplished by knowing you can trust God, not trying to make yourself believe that you can. When you are having a faith (trust) problem don't try to produce more faith, just spend more time with God. I have found, if I have trouble believing, I can relax because I know my relationship with God is still developing.

We understand this perfectly in our earthly relationships. If someone you are just getting to know asks you out for lunch and they are late, how sure are you that they will show up at all? You're not sure because you don't know their character yet. You are just hoping they will not stand you up. When you already know someone well and they are late, you might get a table and order your drinks. You do this because you know their character. They are the kind of person who will keep their word. This simple analogy explains Satan's concerns about you knowing God. God's character is good, and He is absolutely trustworthy. Satan knows if you truly get to know God then it is inevitable that you will trust Him. In this trust you will believe every word He tells you and obey everything He asks you to do.

This is why Satan's target is the knowledge of God. His deception about God will always plant seeds of mistrust in your mind. His plan in the garden was to challenge what God had said. First, he directed Eve's attention to the fact that God would not allow them to eat from every tree. This implied God was withholding something from them. After Eve's answer his response was to contradict what God had said, by telling her she would not die. Furthermore, he lied again by telling her that eating the fruit would make them like God. This was an attack on God's character and His motives. Satan has never changed his approach because it has proven to be very effective.

"Heart knowledge": the knowledge that God is good and wishes to reward anyone who pursues relationship with him.

I want to address the subject of faith a little more because it is a crucial element of our spiritual journey. At times, the concept of faith can seem to have nothing to do with our relationship with God. Hebrew 11:6 actually gives us two requirements of faith, *"But without faith it is impossible to please Him, for he who comes to God must believe that He is, and that He is a rewarder of those who diligently seek him."* The first requirement is to believe that God exists. James 2:19 says that even the demons believe that God exists. This is what I call "The two unbalanced requirements of faith," on **Diagram B**. The first requirement could be met by anyone. I call this head knowledge or mental assent. The second requirement is to believe that God is a rewarder. This is what I call heart knowledge; the knowledge that God is good and wishes to reward anyone who pursues relationship with Him. If there is almost no weight placed on the first requirement, then where does all the significance of faith rest? It rests on heart knowledge, knowing God will reward us out of His goodness. We cannot even please God without this requirement of faith.

The word faith is only used twice in the Old Testament: Deuteronomy 32:20 and Habakkuk 2:4. It is not because the concept is not there, it is just that another word is used instead. That word is trust. If you substitute the word trust for the word faith in any New Testament verse it will greatly enhance your ability to understand the meaning of the passage. The word trust is linked closely to relationship whereas faith can easily become an abstract concept. Faith can easily turn into a work on the part of the believer. If you substitute the word faith for the word trust, the understanding becomes clouded. Try replacing the word trust with the word faith in Proverbs 3:5, have faith in the Lord with all your heart. Trust and faith are one and the same. They are both about relationship; it is only that we perceive trust as being more relational. The problem is that we inadvertently think of faith as something that we must do instead of have. The word trust implies faith by its very nature.

How do I separate my thoughts from me?

One of the biggest lies is that all the thoughts that go through your mind are your own thoughts.

Now we will begin the process of understanding the lies in our minds and how to differentiate them from truth. If you are able to stop reading at this moment, I would like to give you an assignment. I would like for you to make a list of the negative thoughts (lies) that go through your mind. My objective is for you to physically write these thoughts down somewhere. The reason for this assignment is crucial to personal freedom. One of the biggest lies of all is that all the thoughts that go through your mind are your own thoughts. This is simply not true. By separating yourself physically from the lies you write on paper, it will enable you to make a clean break between yourself and the lies. It is crucial that you understand that you and the lies are not one and the same.

No one wants to fight with themselves, but if they realize an enemy is attacking they become inspired to fight!

If you are not able to do this now, please do it as soon as possible. Do not skip this assignment. Later, when you hear the same lies you have heard for years, you will continue to battle against yourself unless you realize the lies are not yours. This is a crucial initial step to freedom, so please do not skip it. No one wants to fight with themselves, but if they realize an enemy is attacking, they become inspired to fight! If the lie, you are a bad mother, has constantly been harassing you, once you write it down, the next time it comes you will not beat yourself up. You will know that it is one of Satan's customized lies just for you, and you will cast it aside like we spoke of earlier.

For those of you who are fortunate enough to have very few negative thoughts, I have a method to generate some for you. Prepare a topic for public speaking and you will have as many negative thoughts as you can handle. The more influence you have with people, the more these negative thoughts (lies) will exponentially increase. Try it out, or remember what you heard the last time you spoke. This will generate some lies for your list.

A thought is not yours just because you think it.

Now, I am going to ask you to do something very strange indeed. You probably shouldn't do this if you are in public. You might want to wait until you get alone, but regardless, still do it. Take your right hand and hold it out in front of you. I would like for you to talk to your hand, so repeat after me: "Hand, everything you pick up is not a part of me." Now take your right foot and hold it out so you can see it. Speak to your foot and say: "Foot, everything you walk on is not a part of me." Now put both hands on your head and repeat after me: "Mind, every thought you think is not a part of me." This is always a lot of fun with a live audience, because I can see that some people are greatly concerned that I am delving into some "new age" ungodly doctrine.

This might appear strange, but is a very practical demonstration to teach you the most freeing of all principles. All of the thoughts that go through your mind are not yours! You are not responsible for generating every thought that comes into your mind. Your mind is a great processor. It can picture a TV show from years ago, it can remember something you learned in the tenth grade, or it can imagine you at a Hawaiian Luau and make up the entire atmosphere. Your mind is a vital part of you, but just like your hand or foot does not make something a part of you by touching it, neither is a thought yours just because you think it.

Understanding this one concept can make it so much easier to fulfill the commandment given in 2 Corinthians 10:5, "...*bringing every thought into captivity to the obedience of Christ.*" This command is much easier to accomplish when we know we are not fighting against ourselves. Some of us, at one time or the other, have become angry and thought of killing someone else. However, because most of us <u>did</u> take that thought captive, we are not in prison. It is similar with the thought of suicide. If you realize that an enemy has planted this lie to get your agreement, you are more inclined to resist the lie instead of cooperating with it.

Chapter 9

How Can I Avoid Being Manipulated?

Is God really good?

God is good and He is only good. He will only be good to you; He will never do anything mean or harmful to you. Anything you have heard contrary concerning God's character is a lie. You could have believed the lie that God is cruel or that He can do both good and bad things. Satan will even use the Bible to try and perpetuate these lies. A passage from the book of Job is often misused for this purpose. Job 1:21 says, *"... The Lord gave, and the Lord has taken away..."* This passage is often used by well-intentioned people as an attempt to explain that some of the bad things that happen to us are sent from God.

I believe they may have unknowingly fallen into one of Satan's deceptive traps. Job later confessed that he did not know what he was talking about, *"You asked, who is this who hides counsel without knowledge? Therefore I have uttered what I did not understand, things too wonderful for me, which I did not know"* (Job 42:3). I believe it is unwise to use the retracted words of a man in extreme anguish to explain the character of God. 2 Corinthians 10:5 clearly shows us that the target of our mutual enemy is the knowledge of God. Have you ever had a testimony of God in a moment of crisis that was less than correct? God sympathizes with our pain and can handle our venting, but Satan will use words spoken in our crisis to advance his cause. It is always in Satan's best interest to defame God's character in order to quench the desire to draw closer to Him. He is not above using the written word of God to achieve his purpose. Any theology, no matter how prevalent, that accomplishes this purpose has mistakenly fallen under the influence of our enemy, the devil.

God is a perfectly loving heavenly father toward you. Jesus died to pay the penalty for your sins so you could be restored into relationship with Him and with His Father. God is no longer holding your sins against you, and has no legitimate reason to punish you in any way. The penalty for your sins was taken by Jesus on the cross (Romans 6:23). If we had to pay for our own sins, we would all be dead. God is no longer holding your sins against you. God's justice will not allow Him to illegally charge you with a crime for which Jesus has already paid the penalty. *"As far as the east is from the west, so far has He removed our transgressions from us"* (Psalm 103:12).

Any thoughts that are attempting to bring shame or condemnation on you are not from God.

Satan is a master at manipulating the guilt over our own sins to destroy our relationship with God. If you are harassed with thoughts of past sins, those thoughts are not from God. Love thinks no evil (1 Corinthians 13:5). This in the Greek means: to keep no account of evil. God, Who is Love (1 John 4:16), keeps no record of your sin. Out of love, the Holy Spirit will speak to you about a present sin, but He does this to spare you the pain of the sin's consequences. His desire is not to shame you, but give you abundant life. Sin is a thief that steals your abundant life, and God's heart is to protect you from the thief.

No matter if it is you personally, a friend, or a family member who is bringing up your past sins, they are not operating on God's behalf. Do not let this strategy of your enemy go undetected. It only takes a little time dwelling on your sin to completely distract you from the knowledge of how much you are loved by God. Any thoughts that are attempting to bring shame or condemnation on you are not from God. God's desire is that you have joy: *"…the joy of the lord is our strength"* (Nehemiah 8:10). Psalm 44:7, speaking of Jesus says, *"You loved righteousness and hated wickedness; therefore God, Your God, has anointed You with the oil of gladness more than Your companions."* If the thought is condemning, shaming, or steals your joy, double check the source because it is not God.

Why is there power in relationship?

Why it is so important to Satan that you be unable to comprehend God's love for you? The knowledge of who loves you is the strength of who you are as a person. I would like you to write down all the people who have loved you, cared about you, or have had a positive influence upon your life.

If your list contains more than a few people, consider yourself extremely blessed. If you could not think of anyone, do not become discouraged. As you come to know the love God has for you it will more than compensate for any human deficits. Here is the point of this exercise. Love makes you strong. Now that you have written this list, I want you to picture what your life would be like if these relationships had never existed. Can you feel how this would drain the strength out of your life? A significant part of Satan's plan against you is to destroy these positive, loving relationships.

Let's look at a Biblical example of how love makes you strong. This is a prayer of the early Christian church which was being persecuted for their faith in Jesus. *"Now, Lord, look on their threats, and grant to Your servants that with all boldness they may speak your word, by stretching out Your hand to heal, and that signs and wonders may be done through the name of Your holy Servant Jesus. And when they had prayed, the place where they were assembled together was shaken; and they were all filled with the Holy Spirit, and they spoke the word of God with boldness"* *(Acts 4:29-31).*

The early church was so effective in spreading the news of Jesus because they were absolutely certain of His love for them.

Knowing God's love intimately produces a certainty about His character. This certainty produces courage. This bold courage, in God, is what advanced the early church so rapidly across the known world even in the face of violent opposition. The above believers had been persecuted, threatened, and told not to preach in Jesus name. The early church was so effective in spreading the news of Jesus because they were absolutely certain of His love for them. Did you notice that they didn't even ask to be delivered from their enemies who were bringing the persecution?

How would this persecution be handled in the modern church today? Most of the time, as soon as something bad happens, we respond with: Lord, please take this away; Lord, why has this happened to me; what's wrong; what have I done wrong; why do I not have enough faith to stop this? The lack of knowledge of God's true love for us produces an inward focus, however the knowledge of God's love produces an outward focus, which is what we see in the early church. This emphasizes the need for a greater understanding of the love God has for us in much of the church today.

Love makes you fearless.

The early disciples were Christ-centered. They were thinking more about proclaiming Him than their own problems. This is how the knowledge of God's love empowers you. Satan is afraid of this God-centered courage. Love makes you fearless. *"There is no fear in love; but perfect love casts out fear, because fear involves torment. But he who fears has not been made perfect in love"* (1 John 4:18). What enemy in their right mind would want to fight a fearless opponent? Not even Satan is that stupid! Satan is so afraid of your becoming fearless, he will do everything he can to push you away from God's love which produces that fearlessness.

How do I know the character of God the Father?

God is full of compassion.

There is a phrase in the book of Psalms that describes the character of God and is repeated many times. I will quickly go over five of them before we explain their meaning. *"But He God being full of compassion forgave their iniquity and did not destroy them"* (78:38). *"But You O Lord, are a God full of compassion and gracious, long suffering, and abundant in mercy and truth"* (86:15). *"The Lord is gracious and full of compassion"* (111: 4). *"He [God] is gracious* and _full of compassion_ and righteous" (112:4). And lastly, "The Lord is gracious and _full of compassion_, slow to anger, and great in Mercy" (145:8). This phrase repeatedly describes God as being <u>full of compassion</u>, but what does this actually mean?

The Hebrew language of the Old Testament is very descriptive. Therefore, we can gain a much broader understanding by looking at the meaning in the original language. The word <u>full</u> means: to be completely satisfied like you had eaten a big meal. The word <u>compassion</u> means: to tenderly caress in a loving way, especially to love, pity, and show mercy. Put together, they mean that God is completely satisfied just like He had eaten a big meal when He is able to tenderly caress you in a loving way; especially to love, pity, and show you mercy. This is the character of God and this is why the lies keep coming: to stop you from knowing a God this in love with you.

If you had an earthly father who was like this, how would you react if someone insulted his character? You would probably get defensive. People who know their God develop a sort of militancy about proving His character. When you really get to know a heavenly Father this good, an attack on His character seems outrageous. The suggestion that He would actually do you harm seems ludicrous. As you mature in His love, you clearly begin to see the cloud of deception that Satan has been able to pull over the eyes of almost everyone. The compassion of God rises in your heart toward those who are deceived. You become one with God's heart of deliverance.

Here is another Old Testament passage that reveals the character of God. "Who is a God like you pardoning iniquity and passing over the transgression of the remnant of His heritage? He does not retain His anger forever, because _He delights in mercy_" (Micah 7:18). I want to focus on what the last phrase "delights in mercy" means in the original language. In Hebrew the word delights means: to be inclined to, to be pleased with, or to desire. The word mercy means: loving kindness. This is clearly telling us that God not only desires to show us His loving kindness, He is also pleased when He is able to do so. This is a fact: what makes God happy is being nice to you. Anything else you have believed about God's character is a lie. What good earthly father is different from this? A good father never wants his children to fail. A good father wants to show them affection. A good father is happy when he can be kind to his children.

How do I know the character of Jesus?

Jesus is moved with compassion.

There is a phrase in the New Testament used repeatedly to describe the character of Jesus. This phrase is distinctly different from the one used to describe God, His Father. *"But when He, Jesus, saw the multitudes He was moved with compassion for them"* (Mathew 9:36). *"And when Jesus went out He saw a great multitude and He was moved with compassion for them and healed their sick"* (Matthew 14:14). In another passage, someone with leprosy confesses to Jesus that he believes Jesus could heal him, but says, *"If you are willing you can make me clean"* (Mark 40:1). *"Then Jesus, moved with compassion, stretched out His hand and touched him, and said to him, I am willing; be cleansed"* (Mark 40:2). God is described as full of compassion and Jesus is described as moved with compassion. This small difference has significant ramifications. In the original Greek the definition of the word moved means: to have the bowels yearn, to feel sympathy, and to have pity. Jesus felt such sympathy and pity for the hurting that He actually felt it in His physical body.

What is the difference between Father and Son if They are both God? If you were to think of God the Father as a cup full of compassion, then Jesus is the overflow of that same cup of compassion poured out on mankind. Jesus is God in action, showing His love for the objects of Their mutual affection: people. Remember, God is completely satisfied when He can show us mercy. Like father, like Son is the perfect description of Jesus.

Through Jesus, God was able to touch the objects of His love.

In one instance it is recorded that Jesus was so satisfied ministering to the people, He forgot to eat. *"... His disciples urged Him, saying, Rabbi, eat. But He said to them, I have food to eat which you do not know. Therefore the disciples said to one another, has anyone brought Him anything to eat? Jesus said to them, My food is to do the will of Him who sent Me, and to finish His work"* (John 4:31-34). Jesus was completely satisfied, just like His Father, when he could tenderly caress in a loving way, especially when He was able to show pity and mercy.

Jesus was able to physically show God's affection. Through Jesus, God was able to touch the objects of His love. God was touching the people through the hands of Jesus. This is why you so often see Jesus laying hands on people and touching them. This gave both He and His Father great joy. At the last Passover meal which Jesus ate with his disciples, it is recorded that John, His disciple, laid his head on Jesus's chest. Jesus loved to touch people. The first lie that I refuted at the beginning of this book was that God is not interested in relating to you. I just gave you more irrefutable evidence that this is completely untrue. We only have to look at Jesus. Jesus even said in John 14:9, *"... He that hath seen Me has seen the Father..."* If you really want to know what God is like, just watch Jesus. Jesus enjoyed physically touching people.

Do I have a co-dependent relationship with any lie?

There is a strange co-dependent relationship that develops between our hearts and the most frequent lies we hear. For example, you may become so accustomed to the voices in your head telling you that you are lazy, you become uncomfortable with the thought of losing that familiarity. Although you would argue with someone who insulted you in this way, you are accustomed to hearing the lie in your own mind. It feels like it is a part of who you are. This is the equivalent of having an older, more comfortable pair of shoes, which may not look as good as new, yet you still prefer them because you are used to how they feel on your feet.

There is an unspoken fear of loss with familiar strongholds.

The comfort derived from these strongholds is that they define who you are and how you should act. They have effectively removed that burden of responsibility from your shoulders. There is an unspoken fear of loss with familiar strongholds. You unconsciously say to yourself that you have believed these lies so long you are not sure who you are without them. Overcoming the victim mentality is a crucial component of being able to break the power of a stronghold. If you agree with the stronghold then you are a victim; if you do not, then you are responsible for your future. Some people never want to take that responsibility. If you have believed the lie that you are stupid then there is no need to apply yourself in study. However, if you reject that lie, who is now expected to open a book? Once you pull down the stronghold, you can no longer allow yourself to be the victim. Understanding God's love will provide the necessary courage you will need to walk in your new-found freedom.

Some of you reading right now did not do the assignment earlier of writing down your negative thoughts. Only about five percent of the students in a classroom setting do the assignment the first time I ask. Ask yourself these questions and be honest. Do I have a fear of actually facing these lies in print? If so, what am I afraid of? Am I so driven to finish this book that I do not want to take the time to write them down? If so, what is driving me? I had one student, after writing them down, get so nervous they immediately destroyed the list. True transformation is about vulnerability in your relationship with God. Do not be afraid to come to God emotionally naked. God's love is the safest place you could ever come for healing. You will never shock God. He already knows what you look like under your fig leaves.

How can I become more childlike?

Our fantasies about true love usually skip the vulnerability factor.

As a teacher I must constantly remind myself that, compared to my eternal heavenly Father, I will always be a child. Children are vulnerable and they are honest. What you see is what you get. I think this is what Jesus meant in Matthew 18:3, *"Assuredly, I say to you, unless you are converted and become as little children, you will by no means enter the kingdom of Heaven."* I am reminded of the words of an old song by The Eagles, "Desperado"[A]: "…you gotta let somebody love you, before it's too late." Our fantasies about true love usually skip the vulnerability factor; but without the possibility of rejection, how would we ever know that love was real. The great news is that you are already accepted in Christ. *"To the praise of the glory of His* grace, *by which He made us accepted in the Beloved"* (Ephesians 1:6). Never fear; your vulnerability with God will always be accepted with open arms.

As children we are born with a desire to be loved for who we are, apart from anything that we do. This involves more than our personalities and actions, it is also what we secretly long for with our dreams and imaginations. There is something in all of us that wants to imagine and dream about anything we want, and have those dreams be accepted. This deep desire has to come from our spirit because it is definitely not from this world. This world is altogether different from the one we longed for it to be. The first thing most of us lose is that childlike belief that a place of total acceptance could exist. This fallen world is like a slap in the face to the innocent belief of unconditional freedom and acceptance. We learn very quickly to tone it down and think in line with what is the expected norm for this world's system.

I am not sure what heaven will be like, but I believe it involves more than an external restoration of our bodies and eternal life. I believe this place of free imagination will be restored, and whatever we can create in our minds will be appreciated for its uniqueness and originality. I also believe that endless possibilities will be a reality as we are completely immersed into the love of God. There is something about our potential here on earth that seems so suffocating in comparison to the freedom in which we were meant to live.

Sin really did cause more than a physical death; it caused a death of possibility and creativity. When someone on earth pushes through these huge obstacles to create something great, the world stands and takes notice. In heaven, I think we will be able to anticipate this kind of originality as part of the blessing and joy of being in the Lord's presence. What will people be able to create with the hindrance of sin removed? *"Eye has not seen, nor ear heard, nor have entered into the heart of man the things which God has prepared for those who love Him" (1 Corinthians 2:9).*

I believe that God wants us to again enter into that place of believing all things are possible, that place we lived in as children. I think faith in His ability transports us to a place outside of our abilities alone, the place where we are really meant to live. One day I was joking with someone about songwriting. I said, "The lyrics are not the hard part for me. I think I could write a song about purple elephants and lyrically it would be fine." I said it flippantly to make the point that I was actually having problems with chord progression. As I got in the car to leave, God said to me, "Could You?" It was like He was challenging me to believe the words which I had just spoken. It was similar to a father encouraging a son and saying, "You can do it!" So I wrote the first verse of the song, "Purple Elephants", in the car on the way home. When I got home I took a nap and wrote the rest of the song as soon as I woke up.

Most of us are unaware that we are imprisoned by a captivity that binds originality and creativity.

I cannot explain how little effort it took to write this song. I was totally shocked by how God led me to such a serious subject by starting with the words purple elephant. It was as if God wanted me to write about a yearning of my heart that I did not even know existed. God wants to restore to you ideas and imaginations that you aren't even aware were stolen. God is an awesome Father. He knows what you need and He wants you to have it all. He wants to deliver you from any and every captivity. Most of us are unaware that we are imprisoned by a captivity that binds originality and creativity. I believe this song will break strongholds binding originality and creativity in your life and you will be stirred up to be child-like once more. I declare that whatever was taken from you must be restored.

You can tap it here or go to
www.TheTruthWins.org/go/PurpleElephants

Purple Elephants

Purple Elephants and rainbow skies,
I'd like to see through a child's eyes.
As time goes on the skies turn grey;
The elephants too, that's the way they came.

Take me back to when I was young,
Teach me all of the songs unsung.
Purple elephants and rainbow skies,
I'd like to see through a child's eyes.

Purple elephants and rainbow skies,
I've been given my Father's eyes.
Rainbows protect me; the elephants too.
My child's not old; he's just like You.

Endless imagination, no concept of time,
As I grow old do I really change,
If You're in me and You stay the same?

I can't grow old, when I live forever,
When I live forever in You.

I can't grow old, when I live forever,
'Cause I live forever in You.

Purple elephants and rainbow skies,
I've been given my Father's eyes.
Purple elephants and rainbow skies,
My child is alive.

Chapter 10

How Do I Fight in This Spiritual War?

How do I know the voice of God?

I am about to give you a practical way to discern whether thoughts that come into your mind are from God or not. Answer the following questions with the most obvious answers. It actually helps if you make the sound! What does a cat sound like? What does a dog sound like? Now, tell me, what does God sound like? Not so easy is it? Let's use the examples of the dog and cat to help answer the question about God. The dog sounds like a dog because it is a dog; likewise, the cat sounds like a cat because it is a cat. Now fill in the blanks: God sounds like _____ because He is _____.

The answer is found in 1 John 4:16, *"And we have known and believed the love that God has for us. God is love, and he who abides in love abides in God, and God in him."* Notice that it does not say that God showed love, or had love. The Bible says God is Love. God sounds like <u>love</u> because He is <u>love</u>. Now that we know the very nature of God, the real question becomes what does love sound like? Just like the dog or cat cannot sound like another animal because it is who they were made to be, neither can God sound like anything but love. You can know for certain what God sounds like based on Who He is. When a thought comes into your mind you will be able to determine whether or not it was spoken by the voice of Love. I am going to show you what Love sounds like, so you will be able to discern what God sounds like. I am going to give you a means by which you may test every thought to determine if it is from God. If you find this technique helpful, then all you will need to do is replicate the process.

...if you know Gods character, then you know what He would say.

"Love suffers long and is kind. Love does not envy. Love does not parade itself. It is not puffed up. Does not behave rudely, does not seek its own, is not provoked, thinks no evil, does not rejoice in iniquity but rejoices in the truth. Love bears all things, believes all things, hopes all things, endures all things. Love never fails..." (1 Corinthians 13:4-8). We clearly see that the Bible says that God is love (1 John 4:16), so, can we replace the word <u>love</u> in verses 4 through 8 with the word <u>God</u>? I believe we can. 1 Corinthians 13:4-8 now becomes a list of God's character traits. God suffers long. God is kind. God does not envy. God does not parade Himself. God is not puffed up. God does not behave rudely. God does not seek His own. God is not provoked.* God thinks no evil. God does not rejoice in iniquity. God rejoices in truth. God bears all things. God believes all things. God hopes all things. God endures all things. God never fails. Here is the key: if you know Gods character, then you know what He would not say!

*When we think of the word "provoke" we immediately think of being provoked to anger. However, in this passage which is giving us the attributes of love (God) I believe Paul is telling us that God cannot be provoked into being anything other than what He is. There is nothing we can do that would cause God to act outside of His character. *"For I am the Lord, I change not"* (Malachi 3:6a). *"Jesus Christ is the same, yesterday, today, and forever"* (Hebrews 13:8). God is not reactionary. Jesus intentionally made a whip out of cords before He drove the money changers out of His Father's house. This was not an act of reactionary anger, but an intentional overturning of their god, the god of money.

Does the Holy Spirit bear witness with you that this list defines the attributes of Gods character? We are now going to take this knowledge of God's character and use it as a weapon. I will show you how to fight a successful spiritual war. We all would like to know how to fight the good fight of faith that Paul charges us to do in 1 Timothy 6:12. Many times spiritual warfare has been mistakenly portrayed as some ethereal concept that we could only hopefully understand after decades in the word of God. This is not true at all. It is a lie from the devil whose main weapon is deception. We should not be surprised that he would tell us lies which basically say that we can't learn how to fight against him because it is too complicated. He will also blame God by claiming He wants you to struggle so you will know Him better. God is the Deliverer, so why would He want to make it more difficult for you to achieve your freedom? That does not make sense because it is a lie. God is not schizophrenic; He either wants you free, or He does not, but it cannot be both.

The outcome of victory in this spiritual war hinges on the discernment of the competing voices in your mind.

The point is not i_f you hear Gods voice; the point is whether you can hear it above all the other competing voices. Jesus explains this well in the next verse, *"Yet they will by no means follow a stranger, but will flee from him, for they do not know the voice of strangers"* *(John 10:5)*. The outcome of victory in this spiritual war hinges on the discernment of the competing voices in your mind. This gives added emphasis to how important it is for the devil to stop you from intimately knowing God. If you know His character; you will know His voice. If you know His voice; you will know the other voices are lies. Knowing God brings clear discernment, and discernment is the supreme defense against deception, Satan's only weapon. If you cannot be deceived and you are obedient to God, you are victorious every single time!

What is the current condition of most human hearts?

The mind is merely the battlefield; the heart is the area of intended occupation.

Any thought that comes into your mind is either true or false. I am not speaking of decision based thoughts such as what to eat or where to go on vacation. I am talking specifically about thoughts that are directed for or against you. These are the thoughts that make you feel blessed or cursed, freed or fearful, fulfilled or depressed, outgoing or withdrawn. These are the thoughts that are coming at you in order to influence your thinking. The Bible is very clear about the source of these negative thoughts. *"For he, Satan is a liar and the father of it"* *(John 8:44)*. The front line of the spiritual battle is drawn in our mind. The battle line is located where these thoughts are accepted or rejected based on their truthfulness. Looking again at **Diagram B**, you can see that if the lies are stopped in the mind they will never reach their intended target, the heart.

The mind is merely the battlefield; the heart is the area of intended occupation. Once a lie is accepted in the human heart it becomes a stronghold which acts like a base of operation. From this point of our agreement (the stronghold), the devil is able to launch covert attacks against you. Once inside the heart the lies become even more effective, since they are no longer resisted. The lies are no longer perceived as being generated from an enemy. They feel like your own, because they agree with previously accepted lies. Any attempt to resist these lies is buffeted back. It's as if you are coming against a fortress. Your own agreement with the lies is reinforcing the strength of this fortress. Before you entered into a relationship with God, the lies were focused on preventing relationship. After you have a relationship with God, they are trying to stop you from fulfilling your purpose in the Kingdom of God.

"This is the condition of most people on earth; they cannot hear the truth that God loves them because of interference from lies going through their minds."

When I am teaching I often do a visual demonstration of the condition of most human hearts. First, I will ask someone to come up from the audience. Then I ask someone in the audience to say the words "I love you" in a normal tone of voice. At the same time, I am gently slapping the person up front on each side of their head, being sure to cup over their ears. I then stop and ask the person in front if they heard what was said. They always reply, "No." This demonstrates the condition of most people on earth; they cannot hear the truth that God loves them because of the interference from lies going through their minds. Sadly, this is equally true of most Christians. Satan will run constant static interference to stop the intended clear reception of God's love.

I sometimes do a second visual demonstration to illustrate the difference between a non-Christian and a Christian. I ask someone to come forward, dress them up in a cowboy hat, and a long equestrian coat called a duster. The coat has both sleeves tied closed so they are unable to use their hands. I ask them to look down so the audience cannot see their face. I explain that this represents a lost person who is completely oblivious to the kingdom of truth. I then have the person look up promptly removing the hat (representing their sin). This demonstrates being saved by receiving the truth. They are now able to receive the truth of God's love.

What about the coat they are still wearing? The long coat represents everything they have ever believed that was not true. But, I thought the person was saved? Salvation sets someone free from the lies that <u>God is not real</u> and <u>God does not love me</u>. However, it does not do away with all of the other lies previously received into the heart. Since the receiving of the former lies was through our free will, it is by our free will they must be rejected.

Just as we were saved by willingly choosing to accept the truth of Jesus' sacrifice; we must also willingly reject all other lies we have believed.

1 John 3:8 says that Jesus came so that he might destroy the works of the devil. Since Jesus said, *"It is finished" (John 19:30)*, we know He completed His mission. He has given us the power and authority to take every thought captive, but it is up to us whether we choose to believe a lie or not.

God never forces decisions on anyone. Just as we were saved by willingly choosing to accept the truth of Jesus's sacrifice, we must also willingly reject all other lies we have believed. The process of removing the coat is what the Bible calls renewing the mind; the shedding of everything that is not from the Kingdom of Truth. The renewal of the mind is essential to developing the freedom needed to walk into our destiny. We do this by rejecting the darkness of deception and embracing who we are in the light of God's truth. By our free choice we make the decision to be as deceived or as free as we want to be.

Why are the arms of the coat bound so that the person is unable to use their hands? This is a very important part of the analogy. We are unable to remove the coat which represents all the past lies we have believed. We were not saved by our own efforts, so in the same way our minds cannot be renewed by our own efforts. But, what are we supposed to do? According to Romans 12:2, we are transformed by the renewing of our mind: *"And do not be conformed to this world, but be transformed by the renewing of your mind, that you may prove what is that good and acceptable and perfect will of God."* Our mind is renewed by our acceptance of the truth, which is exactly the same way we were saved. As we acknowledge the truth and reject the lies, God removes the coat for us. *"If you abide in My word, you are My disciples indeed. And you shall know the truth, and the truth shall make you free"* (John 8: 31-32). God is the Deliverer, but our free will can still agree or disagree with what He is telling us. Agreement allows Him to deliver. Disagreement keeps us in bondage. It is that simple.

How can I speed up my spiritual growth?

The Lord must point out our deception because we are unable to see it.

I have noticed that it is a natural human tendency to desire accelerated spiritual growth. We usually do this by telling God what we feel needs to be changed. This is not our part in the process; our part is to agree with truth. This taking the lead is the very thing that will extend the process. If we have made Jesus our Lord, we need to agree with Him when He reveals something that needs to be changed. God is the Deliverer so He is not extending our captivity, we are. We would be wise to agree with the omniscient Expert and let go of our preconceived ideas of how we would like to be delivered.

There is an old hymn that says it best, "Trust and obey, there is no other way, to be happy in Jesus, but to trust and obey." It is a big mistake to think we can take the coat of old lies off by ourselves. We are not qualified to judge our own heart because it is susceptible to deception. We might indiscriminately remove an imaginative idea as well as a stronghold. We are not qualified to deliver ourselves. What we must do is follow the Lord's leadership.

Being humble enough to receive correction from <u>anyone</u> is a key to our freedom.

You and I are often dealing with years of repeated lies before anyone shows us how they are to be removed. Being humble enough to receive correction from <u>anyone</u> is a key to our freedom. If a friend comes up and says you are selfish or you have unforgiveness, our first thought must be to consider whether or not they might be right. To choose to resist the truth is called self-justification. This is one of the most destructive hindrances to your spiritual growth. We will be discussing the ramifications of self-justification in Chapter 15.

Although we are not qualified to deliver ourselves, we have been given spiritual weapons to take every thought captive. To take every thought captive is to discern whether each thought we have is a truth or a lie, and then to willfully choose to reject the lies. This sounds like a lot of work, but with a little practice it will become a naturally automatic response. You will not be exerting excessive effort to fight these lies forever.

As a personal example, I have heard many lies as I have been writing this book. Here is a small sample: this is too dry, not enough people will care about this, your vocabulary is not very good, and this is too complicated. It was not difficult for me to reject those lies because they did not agree with God's character of love. Once you get the truth of God's true character in your heart, the process becomes simple. And now we are going to practice using our new-found knowledge of Who God really is and how He relates to us.

What are some practical techniques for casting down lies?

Here is a practical application of using the character of God that we found in 1 Corinthians 13 to accurately discern whether a thought is from God. I am going to give you examples of thoughts that could go through anyone's mind. Without looking ahead in the book I would like for you to tell me if these thoughts could be from God. The only limitation I have is that the proof can only come from the character traits of God listed in 1 Corinthians 13:4-8. Here is the List: God suffers long and is kind, God does not envy, God does not parade Himself, God is not puffed up, God does not behave rudely, God does not seek His own, God is not provoked, God thinks no evil, God does not rejoice in iniquity, God rejoices in truth, God bears all things, God believes all things, God hopes all things, God endures all things, and God never fails.

The main reason lies may have been effective in your life is the confusion about their source.

Here is the first thought: you are an idiot. Is it possible that this thought came from God? Someone will always shout out in class, "NO!" But, that is not what I asked them to do. I wanted them to show me proof, from the character list of God above, why that thought cannot be true. God is kind and God is not rude are two of His character traits that stand as irrefutable evidence that God could not send us that thought. Many times there will be more than one piece of corroborating evidence from these verses. God cannot act outside of His character, so it is absolutely impossible for Him to have sent that thought. God's character tells us He would not say this, and these verses describe His character. At this point, you might be thinking that you have been struggling your whole life with negative thoughts and can it really be this simple to remove them. Yes! The reason this is so effective is that it is not a formula, but it establishes a foundation in God's character which cannot fail. <u>The main reason lies may have been effective in your life is the confusion about their source.</u>

Now, let's try another thought: you will never finish, just quit. Can that thought be from God? No! What is our proof? We again have multiple proofs: God hopes all things, God believes all things, God never fails, and God is patient. Any of these character traits of God are proof that He would not say that. There is another way this same thought could come to your mind: you need to change what you are doing or you will never finish. The difference between these two thoughts is that this one has the signature of God on it. It gives you correction and instruction. It is correctional without being condemning. God is never condemning, but He will correct you and there is a big difference between the two. God cannot condemn or shame you because that is not part of His character. God can warn you about a time frame on a task because He cares about you. Always notice the feelings of shame and condemnation; they are red flags to alert you that the devil is the source of the thought.

First, refute the lie based on the character of God Himself. Second, reinforce the strength of your position with more proof of God's character.

Once you have proven that a thought is a lie and not from God, it is always helpful to reinforce your resistance to the lie with additional scriptural truth. What truth would be good to fight against the lie that says you are an idiot? There are many, but I like using 1 Corinthians 2:16, *"For who has known the mind of the Lord that he may instruct Him? But we have the mind of Christ."* If someone has the mind of Christ, then how could they be an idiot? This seems so simple, but when I do this with a live audience, I am always amazed at how much fun people seem to be having. I think it is because in our hearts we know God is good, but we have never understood the simplicity of proving it. Once we have the tools, we act like attorneys in a court case we cannot lose.

This is how you fight spiritual warfare. First, refute the lie based on the character of God Himself. Second, reinforce the strength of your position with more proof from His own words. This is the most effective way to cast down a lie and at the same time strengthen your defenses to keep it out. **The exact same lies will come back** because

Satan is extremely unoriginal! If you can refute a lie once, you can refute it a thousand times. It simply gets easier each and every time.

What would be a good scripture to resist the lie that you cannot finish? *"I can do all things through Christ who gives me strength"* *(Philippians 4:13)*. Someone who can do all things because Christ lives in them, can finish! This understanding of warfare is the exact same one that Jesus used when He was tempted by the devil in the wilderness. In the biblical account there are three recorded temptations and, all three times, Jesus responded by quoting His Father's words. If you will make it a habit to think of a scripture to combat every lie that comes at you, a time will come when this process becomes automatic.

It is imperative that we begin to stop our own repetition of the lies.

Because we are absolutely certain that these lies cannot come from God, then whoever is delivering the lie is not being used by God. Many of you may have told yourself you are an idiot or that you are a quitter. Let me be very direct. If you, or anyone else, is propagating these lies, they are aiding the enemy. We must vigilantly resist being used by the devil in our own life or the lives of others. We may be able to blame the devil for the lies, but often we are the ones repeating the lies he originated. It is imperative that we stop our repetition of these lies. If we are speaking a lie, its source is our heart and the stronghold cannot be destroyed until we renounce it. We have enough coming against us without assisting our enemy in his attempts to destroy us.

Chapter 11

Why Do the Lies Get So Personal?

What are my personally tailored lies?

Any thought that is attempting to steal your hope cannot be from God!

I would like to talk about how personally tailored these lies can become by giving you an example from my own life. I was tormented by this particular lie for nearly twenty years: your situation will not change. It took me a long time to learn how to deal with this lie because, in the natural, things never did change. Unfulfilled dreams stayed unfulfilled. The purpose of this lie was to steal my hope. Since Satan only comes to steal, kill, and destroy, it can be helpful to ask what any lie is attempting to steal, kill, or destroy. Now go back to our list of character traits for God in 1 Corinthians 13:4-8, and tell me how we know the thought that your situation will not change cannot be from God? The answer is self-evident: God hopes all things! What would be a good scripture to fight against an attack on hope? How about Jeremiah 29:11? *"For I know the thoughts that I think toward you says the Lord, thoughts of peace and not of evil, to give you a future and a hope."*

Lies can only steal your hope if they take your eyes off your eternal destiny.

Any thought that is attempting to steal your hope cannot be from God! If we are tormented by hope stealing lies, the situation we are in is not permanent. We will not have the lies in heaven. In other words, no matter what we are going through in this life, it is temporary. God loves you, and His eternal plan for you is a bright and glorious future spent with Him in heaven, despite what happens on this earth. Lies can only steal your hope if they take your eyes off your eternal destiny.

The more you learn to cast down these incoming lies, the more you will realize they are repetitive and unoriginal. God, as the Creator, gave mankind a creative personality. However, Satan's rebellion seems to have impaired his ability to be creative; his imagination is perverted toward destruction. He must get someone to agree with him in order to distort their agreement for his purpose. He is only effective because of the repetitive use of his only weapon: deception. Repetition, by its very nature, can improve your ability in any activity. However, repetition does not make you smarter, only more skillful. Satan, with his repertoire of repeated lies, has become a very skilled liar, but that does not make him wise. John 8:44 says that he is the father of lies which means he is the originator of deception and his entire kingdom consists only of lies. The devil's familiarity with his weapon of deception, and his use of it, is his only expertise.

Why is understanding the manipulation of shame important?

The reason God cannot remind you of a past sin is because He does not keep a record of your past sins.

The next lie that we are going to look at is a strategy which is custom tailored to fit each individual. Let's consider another deceptive thought. Remember your answer to the following question can only come out of 1 Corinthinans 13:4-8. If you heard a thought in your head that reminds you of a past sin for which you have already repented, can that thought be from God? No! Why? Verse five says that love thinks no evil. This accurately translates to: love keeps no account of wrongs against it. The reason God cannot remind you of a past sin is because He does not keep a record of your past sins. What additional verse would be good to reinforce our resistance to this type of lie? *"As far as the east is from the west, so far has He [God] removed our transgressions from us"* (Psalm 103:12).

This type of lie is meant to bring shame, and shame, as we have seen, is a very effective tool of Satan. Any thought that brings you shame is not from God. The Holy Spirit does not bring shame. He only reveals ongoing sin in your life for the purpose of your acknowledgement and repentance. This is a gentle reminder to keep your heart free, but there is no shame attached. If there is shame involved in a thought, it is not from God. Godly <u>conviction</u> is the feeling of knowing you have not acknowledged a sin which the Holy Spirit has brought to your attention. <u>Condemnation</u> is an attempt by Satan to utilize your past sin to demean your worth. *"God did not send His son into the world to be its Judge and to condemn the world, but to be its Savior and rescue it!"* (John 3:17 TPT). God is never condemning because He set your worth and, no matter what you do, your worth is constant in God's eyes. Condemnation is an attempt to devalue you. Why would God devalue someone on which He Himself set such a high value?

If you or anyone else brings up a past sin, this is not operating on behalf of God's kingdom. It does not matter if it is your husband, wife, father, mother, or best friend. Anyone who would bring up something that has been separated from you as far as the east is from the west is not displaying the character of God. Your sins are not recorded anymore; they were dealt with at the cross. Once Jesus said, "It is finished," God's righteous judgment against sin was satisfied. If you should find yourself dwelling on your past sins, realize you have gone to the kingdom of lies to get your information. Your sins are not listed in the Kingdom of Truth.

One way to fight these attacks is to separate yourself as much as possible from anyone who continually brings up your past sins. This can be very difficult with loved ones. However, shame is such a powerful weapon against you that, temporarily, it might be your best option. Until you have mastered casting down these lies, it would be best to eliminate the source of as many as possible, even if it means physically removing yourself from some relationships. Pray and ask the Holy Spirit to lead you in this area. It is best not to make hasty decisions, but to wait on God's leading.

Jesus paid the full price for all sins; our shame is nothing more than selfish pride.

The most difficult type of shame is not that which is originated by others, but the shame we put upon ourselves. Some of us, at the very least, find it difficult to accept Jesus's full payment for sins. We feel compelled to contribute to His work on the cross by adding the shame we feel over our sins. Jesus paid the full price for all sins; our shame is nothing more than selfish pride. If we allow this shame to rule our lives, we are exalting ourselves above the work Jesus did on our behalf. Shame is a hideous sin because it masks itself as humility when, in actuality, it is the opposite, spiritual pride. Dwelling on what we have done in the past dishonors the free gift of being born again into the kingdom of God. Shame is such a powerfully deceptive lie because it is such an easy sell to our self-centered human nature.

<u>Warning:</u> beware of any feelings that magnify your guilt. You are forgiven, regardless of your feelings. You must boldly stand on the finished work of Jesus when these lies come or the strategy of shame will suck the joy out of your life. Remember, the joy of the Lord is your strength.

Rejoice in Jesus for He destroyed the record of what you have done. He has slain the dragon and rescued you. Glorify God in the overwhelming strength of your Savior. He has never been defeated and He has never won half a victory. He is completely victorious over your sins. He is Christus Victor (Christ the Victor).

In general terms, if the thoughts coming at you are causing you to focus on yourself then they are not from God. The answer again is found in 1 Corinthians 13:5, "...*love does not seek its own*". True Love, which is God, does not think of Himself. The more we are like God, the more we will not be thinking about ourselves. Shame focuses all attention on us and is in total opposition to the selfless heart of God. Don't let this false humility attach to your heart. It is probably the craftiest of all deceptions.

Shame is tricky because it agrees with the guilt we <u>feel</u> from our former sin nature, but we are no longer in our old sin nature. "*Therefore, if anyone is in Christ, he is a new creation: old things are passed away; behold all things are become new" (2 Corinthians 5:17).* We no longer are to agree with guilt and shame. We are freed from them. Jesus, as we saw, despised our shame and removed it at the cross. We no longer need to listen to our old feelings; we are guided by God's Own Spirit of Truth Who lives in us. *"However, when He the Spirit of Truth, has come, He will guide you into all truth; for He will not speak on His own authority, but whatever He hears He will speak; and He will tell you things to come" (John 16:13).* Choose to listen to the voice of His Spirit, not the voice that makes you feel comfortable!

What does true repentance look like?

True repentance purposely refuses to dwell on the sin itself, but on Jesus who has paid the penalty to take it away.

What does true repentance look like? Repentance is agreement at the heart level evidenced by a change in behavior. True repentance purposely refuses to dwell on the sin itself, but on Jesus who paid our penalty in order to remove it from us. Repentance should be relatively fast. To people who do not understand the grace of God offered through Jesus's sacrifice on the cross, it may appear to be insincere. A healthy mature Christian will remain Christ-centered even if they sin, yet they will not abuse the free gift of God's grace by planning to sin. They will not abuse the fact that forgiveness has already been provided for their sin. Godly repentance is quick because the agreement with the Holy Spirit's conviction is quick. This is an indication of someone who is obediently listening to God's voice. However, a truly repentant person is not flippant about the forgiveness because they understand the magnitude of the price paid for their rescue.

Why is true repentance so significant to our spiritual growth? As we grow in our relationship with God, He will lovingly bring up our sins so our developing relationship can be free from sin's effects. As our relationship deepens, we become a clearer channel of His love toward others. God's desire is that we have integrity; that we are the same in mind, heart, and body. Think of yourself as God's pipeline of life-giving water directed toward others. If there is no confusion between your mind and heart, the compassion of God's love will easily flow through you. When our hearts and minds are in conflict, there is internal opposition blocking the flow of God's love to others. We do not have to be afraid of God's judgment on our sins. Jesus took our judgment for sin on the cross. However, God hates sin because it destroys our relationship with Him and with those He would like to demonstrate His love to through us.

Creativity, stimulated by our freed imagination, will begin to flourish.

As integrity grows within us, the division that previously existed between our heart and mind is eroded by love. This produces the unexpected byproduct of creativity. Creativity, stimulated by our freed imagination, will begin to flourish. Our true personality, without sin, becomes transparent before the Lord. This transformation takes you into your true destiny by growing your understanding into the realization of who you were uniquely made to be. Sin destroys intimacy and, without intimacy, there is no reproduction. Without intimacy with God, there is no creativity of new life produced within us. As we become comfortable being ourselves with God, without the shame of sin, that is when we reproduce the most in God's kingdom. But, what does this look like?

Why does being yourself release the life of God?

I have found that the freer you are, the more God talks to you according to your personality. This is because God loves everything about you. He loves your smile, your gestures, and every single aspect that makes up your personality. He knows what you like and He loves relating to you in a way that you will enjoy. Personally, I can be rather scattered in my thinking with my mind functioning like a jigsaw puzzle whose pieces appear not to connect. I have found that God will speak to me many times by linking these apparently unrelated pieces. At times, this can be hilarious. Let me give you some examples.

Really good relationships are where both participants are having a lot of fun being in each other's company.

I was driving along one day proudly thinking about how I was able to think outside of the box. I also was thinking how nice it was not to be trapped by the in-the-box kind of thinking. Instantly, I kid you not, I heard an oriental voice in my mind say, "There is no box." I knew it was God, because what He said was profoundly true in every way. The fact that He said it in that voice was just funny. I cannot ever think of that and not become joyful.

Nehemiah 8:10 says, *"…the joy of the Lord is your strength."* Really good relationships are where both participants are having a lot of fun being in each other's company. I am sorry to say that you seldom see a marriage relationship like this, but when you do, it is almost impossible not to appreciate it. I have observed this kind of light heartedness in married couples and overheard people remark, "Are they married?" We should desire people to be amazed at how carefree we are in our relationship with God.

When God told me there is no box, He was trying to get me to second guess the parameters I had set around myself and others. God saw me with no limits. God has no limits on your potential. For a minute think of how many people you expect to influence for good in your lifetime. Who set that limit? You did. God wants everyone blessed by the unique qualities that only you possess. God is like the proud Father Who would like to show you off to everybody. Even though God is having fun with you in the relationship, it is still reproducing His heart of truth and freedom.

God will sometimes talk to me through old rock song lyrics. I'm not sure why he does that. While growing up I must have stored them in my head, and I guess it's what He has to work with. Here is a funny example. For two weeks I had been singing a one line lyric from a Peter Frampton[A] song; "I want you to show me the way." The entire time I was not sure why, because I had not heard the song in about ten years. I came home one day and took a book off my shelf called "The Art of War"[B], which was written by Sun Tzu, a Chinese military strategist from 200 B.C. I randomly flipped open the book and was shocked to see that Sun Tzu was giving a definition of "The Way". For two weeks I had been singing a one line lyric from a rock song written in 1975 and then I opened a book from 200 B.C to see the answer. Sun Tzu's definition of "The Way" is: when a commander and troops are unified in heart and purpose. According to Sun Tzu, if this happens on the battlefield, the army cannot be defeated. God had answered a cry of my heart with a profound truth. To be victorious I must be one in heart and purpose with Him.

Without even knowing it, I had been praying that God would show me how to wage a good warfare in my life for His Kingdom. Instead of calling this praying in the Holy Spirit, I jokingly call it praying in Peter Frampton. To me that was funny. I was amazed and grateful that God would link the random inventory of my mind to show me something very significant. God is also aware of my scattered thought process, so He did it in a way I will never forget.

When you are free to be yourself is when God will use you the most, with the least amount of effort on your part.

God knows everything about you. He knows the TV shows you watched as a child. He knows everything about the home you grew up in. He knows what pets or even the stuffed animals you had. God will talk to you in any way imaginable to keep the relationship fun and lively. God is not a deep bass voice booming out of the clouds from a movie scene. His desire is to enjoy all of you and for you to get to know the real God who loves you completely. You can relax in your relationship with God. Jesus has dealt with sin, and you are free to be yourself with the God who loves you. I have found the more relaxed I get in the relationship, the more childlike and silly I become. When you are free to be yourself is when God will use you the most with the least amount of effort on your part. My next story exemplifies this perfectly.

While attending Charis Bible College, I was asked to travel with a ministry team to a conference to be a prayer partner. This is someone who helps with individual prayer requests after teaching sessions. Our group was staying in the same large hotel where the conference was being held. The night before the conference began, we were waiting to get on the elevator on the tenth floor when I noticed a couple at the end of the hall. The young man, mid-twenties, went into the room while his female friend remained outside. She made a comment, "Oh, that's my birthday." She was referring to the gentlemen's room number of 1023. I overheard this right before I got on the elevator to go to the first night of the conference.

The following night was a great session and many people came forward for physical as well as emotional healing. When I left, I was on an emotional high from being used by God to help so many people. I had truly released the burden of the people to God and, while praying, some of the counseling had been extremely humorous. As I got off the elevator on the tenth floor, I saw the same couple repeating the scenario where he entered the room and she stayed in the hall.

This is the conversation I had with God, "Can I, God? Is it ok to do this?" I felt like God said I could do whatever I wanted. The young girl was about thirty feet from me when I looked at her with a completely stoic face and said, "Is your birthday October 23rd?" I cannot fully explain how quickly her expression changed when I, a complete stranger, knew her birthday. I was laughing so hard inside I could hardly stand it. For a brief moment I considered continuing the ruse by generic comments that might apply to anyone, such as, "And you desire to be wealthy." I could not contain myself, however, and proceeded to tell her and her boyfriend the story.

What happened next demonstrates why God wants you to be yourself in all situations. As we were all on the elevator going back down to the lobby for something to eat, the couple opened up and shared their story. They were from different parts of the country and had previously met at a similar conference. They both were considering attending Bible college and I was able to share with them vital information about employment opportunities in the area near the college. We had a great conversation which lasted about twenty minutes, and was mutually encouraging to all of us. None of this would have taken place if I had not wanted to play a practical joke on the young lady. God taught me a lesson that night that I have shared many times with others. God uses you the most when you are free to be yourself, not what you think you should be. In your freedom other people are helped and set free.

Satan wants you religious and proper, following the rules. God wants you free and joyful, following your heart. God is not as stoic as we have been led to believe. I think this lightheartedness might have been a contributing factor to why the religious leaders of Jesus's day hated Him so much. They were following the rules, and He was following His heart. They were not enjoying their ministry to the people, and Jesus was having a great time. But worst of all, Jesus's "irreverent" methods were drawing huge crowds, while their apparent "reverence" was keeping the crowds away in droves. Can anyone say envy!

[A]"Show Me The Way" by Peter Frampton. From the album Frampton Comes Alive! A&M SP 3703. 1976

[B]The Art of War ©1988, 1989, 1996, 2000 by Thomas Cleary. Published by Shambhala Publications, Inc. Boston, Massachusetts

Section 3

Knowing Your God Image

Chapter 12

Why Should I Lose My Self-image?

What is self-image?

As we delve further into the issues of the human heart, I need to remind you again of a lie that you will most likely hear. The lie will be: this is too introspective. For extra religious authority, it may additionally have: as Christians we are to be focused on others not ourselves. I love that last part because it almost sounds like the devil is promoting self-sacrifice. Our supposed introspection is only for the purpose of exposing deception so we may walk in the liberty that is ours in Christ Jesus. You cannot lead someone to a place you have never been. Free people set people free precisely because they know the path out of captivity. By now, I hope you can easily see that any attempt to steal that freedom is from our mutual enemy, Satan.

One day, while walking down the hall at Bible college, I asked God an innocent question: "God, how come I understand so much?"

This was not out of pride, but out of humility as I realized that revelation was coming to me much faster than my own personal intelligence could explain. I immediately heard this answer in my mind: "You are losing your self-image." That had to be God, because I did not have the mental capacity to answer myself with such a profound answer.

That one word from God will account for most of the revelation in the remainder of this book. Unless we become as little children, we will not inherit the kingdom of God. One outstanding characteristic of children is that they ask questions. Always have the things that you care about before the Lord in questions, patiently waiting for the answers, and you will never lack revelation in your life. Be sure to look at **Diagram C,** "Losing Your Self-Image", as I explain the revelation further.

The extent to which you do not believe what God believes about you, is the extent to which you have been deceived about yourself.

Self-image means: your concept of yourself (self-perception). So, what did God mean by, "You are losing your self-image"? I will explain with two questions. The first is: when you see yourself, what do you see? The second is: when God sees you what does He see? When the answers to both questions are the same, then, and only then, are you completely free. The extent that you do not believe what God believes about you, is the extent to which you have been deceived about yourself.

What God meant by His statement was that I was losing the wrong image of myself, and I was beginning to see myself the way He does. Deceptions I had held about myself were disappearing; clarity was developing in my heart, causing me to see myself as I

Absolute Truth

Eye of Love

I John 1:5

Foundation:

When God sees you what does He see?

God's Image

1 Cor. 13:4-8

Who you are

Your Heart Leads You

Prov. 16:9 God will lead you in how to see yourself.

Jer. 17:9,10—don't trust your own heart. Trust God's heart for you.

Deceitful—tracked, crooked, polluted

Ways—road, trodden path, course of life

Agreeing with God's truth and not your own self-image will clean the trash out of your life.

Jer. 29:11 (Amplified) - Uniqueness of Individual

Luke 11:34-35

Total Deception

Eye of Evil

John 10:10

When you see yourself what do you see?

Self Image

Prov. 23:7

What you do

Tactics Against You

James 3:16—envy, selfishness

2 Cor 10:12—power in comparison, false identities through false standards, minimulization, self—justification

Matt. 20:1-16 Focus verse 15—jealousy and envy.

How do you feel when someone gets a lot of money?

Diagram C

really am from God's perspective. I had already been teaching on being the bride of Christ, therefore my worth to God was beginning to penetrate into my heart. It is absolutely crucial that we learn our worth in God's eyes.

On the left side of **Diagram C** we have the Kingdom of Truth. If God who created us believes something to be true about us, then it is true. If we believe differently, we have been deceived by the kingdom of lies on the right. The further someone walks away from truth the closer they get to the kingdom of darkness, becoming more and more deceived. Their life may become senseless, and often they will make decisions that seem totally irrational.

Have you ever known someone who was making bad decisions that were causing them personal harm? As a friend, you may have tried explaining how to be free from this self-destructive behavior, but they were unable to comprehend what you were saying. These people are far away from seeing themselves the way God sees them. They have been deceived about their value in God's eyes. We want to be to the far left point on the scale. We want our self-image not to be from our vantage point, but from God's. We want to lose our self-image and have it replaced with God's image of us. How God sees us is true and as we embrace that truth, our full potential is realized.

God is always thinking that you are going to pull it off, make it happen, and be all that you can be.

I explained earlier that the attributes of love in 1Corinthians 13:4-8 are a list of character traits for God. In verse seven it says that love, *"bears all things, believes all things, hopes all things, endures all things."* This is how God, Who is Love, sees you. When God looks at you He sees your full potential, not just at present, but what you were made by Him to be. He sees your character at its fullest; literally, everything you could be. God sees your future as if you had already lived it. That is the only way God sees you because He hopes all things and He believes all things. When it says in verse eight that love never fails, it means God will never stop thinking of you this way. God is always thinking that you are going to pull it off, make it happen, and be all that you can be. That is all He ever sees. It is just part of His personality, and He cannot be any other way.

Why do most of us believe that God thinks differently toward us? You have been reading long enough for the answer to be obvious: lies. Do you remember the target of the kingdom of lies? From 2 Corinthians 10:5 we read, *"...against the knowledge of God."* Just like an earthly father might ask a toddler to jump from a step so he can catch him, that is how trusting you can be with your heavenly Daddy. There can be such unwavering trust that the toddler will sometimes jump before the Dad is ready. In this kind of relationship you can imagine anything is possible, and you believe your Dad can do anything. Well, it just so happens your Heavenly Daddy <u>can</u> do anything. Don't be afraid to jump. This is the oneness in heart with God that is unconquerable in war. This terrifies the devil.

How can I see through God's eyes of love?

Examples of how God sees our potential are all through the Bible. In Judges 6:11-12, when Gideon is hiding in a winepress so his enemies will not find him, God addresses him, *"The Lord is with you, you mighty man of valor."* Does God know Gideon is hiding? Why then would He address him that way? Since God cannot lie, the only answer is that this is how He sees Gideon.

If God sees Gideon that way, then it must be true. The way you and I are seeing and judging Gideon is not who he really is. We are judging by his outward appearance, which we are not supposed to do. *"...For the Lord does not see as man sees; for man looks at the outward appearance, but the Lord looks at the heart"* (I Samuel 16:7b). Even though Gideon himself does not know who he is, that does not alter the fact that God knows. Gideon's view of himself has been distorted by the kingdom of lies, so he is acting out of a believed lie (stronghold) in his heart. God broke the stronghold with the truth. A few minutes later God reinforces the truth of how He sees Gideon in Judges 6:14, *"Then the Lord returned to him [Gideon] and said, 'Go in this might of yours, and you shall save Israel from the hand of the Midianites. Have I not sent you?'"* God sees the potential in all of us that no one else can see.

God uses people to set people free. Just because you are the one in front does not make you vain, just obedient!

There is no telling how many lies Gideon had heard up to this point in his life attempting to make him feel weak and helpless. Why? Because he was the one God was going to use to save the nation. God, by His Spirit, had probably sown the truth of Gideon's greatness somewhere in his heart as a child. I wonder if Gideon had daydreamed about saving his nation from all their enemies. I believe this is true because of how quickly this apparently fearful man believed God. I think Gideon had heard the truth before, but like most of us, thought he was making it up. Some well-intentioned person probably called it a vain imagination. Has someone ever said that to you? If the outcome of your imagination is that people are set free and God gets the glory, it is not a vain imagination. God uses people to set people free. Just because you are the one in front does not make you vain, just obedient!

But, something must have changed on the inside of Gideon because, when he came out of that winepress, he did not hide any more. He now believed who he really was: a mighty man of valor. He continued in the word that God gave him. John 8:31-32 is the key to staying free: *"If you <u>abide</u> in My word, you are My disciples indeed. And you shall know the truth, and the truth shall make you free."* Gideon chose to <u>stay in the truth</u> of what God said about him instead of going back to his familiar lies. Staying in God's truth is how we are able to walk in God's heart of deliverance.

If God has ever given you a word or vision for your future, it is still true. If you want to find your place in this life, you have to go back and pick up the vision. It does not matter if you have not thought about it since you were ten years old, just go back and pick up the vision. In your heart there is a life that you long for, that you know you were meant for. Where you will find your fulfillment is in the individually unique word that God spoke to your heart.

I was taught growing up that the word referred to in John 8:31-32 is the written word of God. Although I understand the importance of the Bible, it has been what God has spoken to me personally, either through the Bible or in agreement with it that has changed my life. What you must grab hold of is the importance of what God tells you personally. It may not be an exact quote from the Bible, but it absolutely cannot contradict God's written word.

God has been directing you all along, even before you knew who He was. *"A man's heart plans his way, but the Lord directs his steps"* (Proverbs 16:9). Notice, your heart is the part of you that is doing the planning, not your mind. Your heart is planning, but the problem with that leading system is it can get lies (strongholds) in it. If you heard the lie that you're not smart enough for college, and you believed it in your heart, guess what your heart plans for you not to do. That's right, go to college.

The Lord will direct you where to go for education, or anywhere else for that matter, if you chose to believe His plan for you in spite of any lies you are or have been hearing. In any life situation God is talking. The question is whether or not you can hear Him above all the other competing voices. To Gideon's credit, he was open to God's direction, and rejected all of the previous lies. With our agreement, God's direction supersedes all of our previously believed perceptions! If you are ever tempted to resist God's direction, picture what Moses's life would have been like on the backside of the desert if he had not agreed with God's plan. Or, you can picture Gideon hiding from his enemies for the rest of his life. Many believers may never know the fulfillment they could have had by just agreeing with God's plan for their life, no matter how impossible it may seem.

Why is the foundation of self-image so weak?

You just need to improve your self-image. This is one of many statements responsible for an entire section at the book store called Self-Help. Much of the focus in this section is an attempt to improve your self-image. I would like to personally challenge the entire concept of self-image as defined by most authors. The main objective of these books is to attempt to improve the way you see yourself. However, they do so without ever dealing with the core issue of why you were created in the first place. When you realize you were created to be loved by God, the knowledge of your true identity obliterates any self-image problem.

A self-image problem is a value (worth) problem. People who have a strong self-image believe they are valuable.

The strength of how you see yourself is based on who loves you. If you think no one cares; you see yourself with little value. But, if you are absolutely certain someone cares, your value or image is no longer in question. A self-image problem is a value (worth) problem. People who have a strong self-image believe they are valuable. An object is worth the price that was paid for it. You were purchased with the life of Jesus Christ. You are so precious in God's eyes that your worth is above any monetary value. This is the truth. Anything you have ever heard contradictory to this is a lie.

The world's system of self-image (value) is based on performance or appearance. The entire foundation of that system is comparison. Realizing that you are a one-of-a-kind creation destroys the comparison used by this world's system of value. We will address the issue of comparison in depth in Chapter 13. But for now, suffice it to say, it is not the foundation of God's system. God's unconditional love and acceptance is the foundation of God's kingdom.

How can I establish the foundation of love?

The love of God is the only stable foundation for your self-worth.

Trying to build your value or self-image on something other than the love of God can be likened to constructing a building on a weak foundation. The love of God is the only stable foundation for your self-worth. When teaching, I use this analogy. I say that the floor I am standing on represents the solid foundation of the love of God. Then, I pull out a rocking chair and I stand in it. When I am on the floor, I am very stable and it is difficult to knock me over. However, once I am standing in that rocking chair, I demonstrate that someone, with just the push of one finger at the top of the chair, can easily cause me to fall. Deception, many times, is attempting to get us to shift off the sure foundation of the love of God and onto a weaker foundation. The devil is aware that once we are on this weaker foundation, any crisis will cause us to be vulnerable during his future attacks.

When you fail in some area and it takes a while to forgive yourself, you can be certain you are on the wrong foundation.

Some of these alternate foundations can be extremely deceptive because they are not bad, in and of themselves, unless we make them the foundation for our self-worth. Some of you reading have the foundation of your self-worth in the belief that you are a good mother or a good father. To be a good parent is a very noble goal, but when this is the basis for your identity, it is very unstable. Once you have altered your foundation, it is like standing up in the rocking chair. It won't take much interference to "rock" your world. The moment you do something a good parent would not do, your self-image will fall apart. All you have to do is yell at the children and you will torment yourself with the guilt and shame for days.

So, how do you know if you are on the wrong foundation? The answer is very simple. When you fail in a particular area and it takes a while to forgive yourself, you can be certain you are on the wrong foundation. If you yell at the children and cannot get over it quickly, your self-worth is in your parenting skills and not in God's love for you. This is true for any area in life. If I deliver a poor teaching, and cannot get over it quickly, my unstable foundation is: I am a good teacher. If I make a bad play in a game and cannot get over it quickly, my unstable foundation is: I am a great ball player.

Your self-image, unless it completely agrees with God's image, is a distorted view of reality.

There is nothing wrong with excelling at teaching or athletics, as long as my self-worth is not derived from my skills, but something more solid. How many people have committed suicide after stock market crashes? If their value had been based on God's love that would have never entered their minds. They were immeasurably valuable, with or without their portfolio, but they had been deceived into believing otherwise in their heart. They took action based on what they believed to be true in their heart, totally oblivious to God's image of them. Your self-image, unless it completely agrees with God's image, is a distorted view of reality. It is a totally unstable foundation.

If you feel unable to forgive yourself for any action, you may have been deceived into believing your self-worth is based on your performance in that particular area. This is an easy lie for Satan to get us to believe because most of this world operates on conditional acceptance, and the foundation of conditional acceptance is performance. Most of us learn early on that if we do well we will be loved more, if we don't do well we will be loved less. Rarely do we meet anyone who operates outside of this system of conditional acceptance.

In God's kingdom, you are loved because you are valuable irrespective of your performance. Satan will take this performance trap and use it to destroy your personal relationship with God. He may use religious duties to deceive you by shifting your focus to your actions for God, rather than your relationship with God. This kind of foundation shifting can even have a daily Bible study as the source of your self-worth. If it is difficult to forgive yourself when you miss a daily Bible reading, then you are off the true foundation. God loves you if you never read the Bible again! God's love is outside of all qualifications. God loves you, period. Reading and studying the Bible is of great benefit, but the motivation should be to know more about the God Who loves you, not to keep up your overly spiritualized self-image.

When your foundation is based on God loving you, you act differently when you sin. Instead of trying to punish yourself with shame, you take ownership of your fault because you know God has already forgiven you. You thank Him for His sacrifice, thank Him for His forgiveness, and then move on with your relationship with Him. When you beat yourself up over your sins, it is a clear indication that you have shifted your foundation off of God's love and onto your own performance. *"For no other foundation can anyone lay than that which is laid, which is Jesus Christ" (1 Corinthians 3:11).* The true foundation is said to be Christ. I believe that this specifically refers to the selflessness of Christ to endure the crucifixion on our behalf. Christ's willingness to lower Himself in order to raise us up is the overwhelming evidence of God's love for us (Philippians 2:5-11). If you have an understanding that is grounded in God's love, you are not easily deceived into shifting your foundation onto your own performance.

How do I have a clear conscience?

"The lamp of the body is the eye. Therefore, when your eye is good, your whole body also is full of light. But when your eye is bad, your body also is full of darkness. Therefore take heed that the light which is in you is not darkness. If then your whole body is full of light, having no part dark, the whole body will be full of light, as the bright shining of a lamp gives you light" (Luke 11:34-36). I believe the eye this passage is referring to is the conscience. The

New Testament word for <u>conscience</u> is defined as: co-perception or moral consciousness. The word <u>good</u> is also translated: singular or clear. So when your conscience, the part of you that perceives good and evil, is singular or clear of obstructions, all of you can be full of the truth and light of God.

Your conscience is like the screen on which you project all your thoughts and actions for judgment, but the screen can become clouded by the lies in your heart. So, how do you have a clear conscience? The key word is humility. Being humble enough to submit to the Lord's leadership and to receive correction is vital to maintaining a clear conscience. Sincerely asking yourself if you could be wrong and being willing to receive correction is absolutely essential.

Pride can disguise itself as self-protection. We can be afraid to admit we are wrong because we hate feeling vulnerable and apparently weak. However, in this place of weakness we have the humility God needs to flood our conscience with the light of more truth. The stronghold of self-protection is driven out of our life in the same way a single candle destroys the darkness of an entire room. At this point we are abandoning the false ideas we have embraced about our identity. This is done simply by being receptive to the light of truth needed to dispel the darkness and set us free.

If a clear or singular conscience can bring the light of truth to the whole body, then an evil or distorted conscience can bring the darkness of deception to the whole person. This explains the apparent lack of conscience in someone who does atrocious acts of evil without remorse. Their conscience has gone completely dark, meaning that their body also is full of darkness. The foundation of this negative downward spiral is the pride inherent in a person who refuses correction.

Why should I agree with my adversary?

Don't feel any need to practice what I am about to tell you until you have a very firm understanding of God's love for you. The point I want to make is that a clear conscience is achieved by agreement with truth, no matter its source. The lies directed at you are most effective when they contain some truth. A lie is actually more dangerous when it is mingled with truth because it is so much more readily accepted by our conscience. Satan could accuse me of being selfish, which I would test against the truth of my life, and judge as false. He could make further accusation by telling me that in that meeting yesterday I was totally selfish, I was talking too much about myself and did not even care about the people who needed prayer. But, was any part of his accusation true?

As mature believers, it is crucial to break apart a lie to dissect it for any evidence of truth. I realize I am not totally selfish or I would not be spending so much time helping people, but did I talk too much about myself and ignore the needs of the people? It is important to pray for the discernment that is needed to separate the truth from the lie. More than likely, I did not ignore the people, but I could have spent more time with them. The scriptural foundation for this is found in Matthew 5:25-26, *"Agree with your adversary quickly, while you are on the way with him, lest your adversary deliver you to the judge, the judge hand you over to the officer, and you be thrown into prison. Assuredly, I say to you, you will by no means get out of there till you have paid the last penny."*

If a lie has enough partial truth in it to expose a weakness, then admit the weakness and change.

When we are attacked our automatic response is to fight back by rejecting the entire lie. As we become more comfortable in our acceptance by God, we can relax and not be so defensive. In the comfort of this acceptance we can accept the truth for what it is. Always agree with the truth, no matter its source. A lie usually contains some truth. You can use this knowledge to your advantage. Allow the partial truth hidden in the lie to expose your weakness; then admit the weakness and change. To me this is what is meant by agreeing with your adversary. To not agree with truth, no matter the cost, is the equivalent to being thrown into a prison of self-deception. Until we agree with the truth that may have been in the lie, we will never get out of our prison of deception.

The application of this technique should only be utilized once you are sure you have a full revelation of your acceptance by God. If you are not there, put this concept on the shelf for later. Listen to God and go with what He tells you in your heart, through the Holy Spirit. You are a truth seeker. We must get the attitude that even if a donkey tells me the truth, I will agree. (For a truth-telling donkey see the story of Balaam in Numbers 22.)

Once we have a clear conscience, there is an incredible amount of revelation that God will send our way in order to help others through the process. Remember God's answer to why I was understanding so much: "You are losing your self-image." Having a God-image causes you to understand so much more through the power of relationship. Therefore, I boldly say that improving your self-image is utter foolishness. Completely replacing it with God's image is the only way to experience the freedom God intended for you.

What was Jesus's self-image?

"This is My beloved Son, in whom I am well pleased."

What kind of image did Jesus have of Himself? Although I believe Jesus already knew this, God confirms it again in Matthew 3:17. *"And suddenly a voice came from heaven, saying, 'This is My beloved Son, in whom I am well pleased'."* Do you realize this is the only image of Himself that Jesus ever had? What would it be like to have never had a poor self-image? Lies never penetrated the heart of Jesus because He was assured of His position as God's beloved Son.

Since we are now in Christ, what is God's image of us? You are God's beloved son or daughter in whom He is well pleased. There is a supernatural place of being able to see yourself from God's perspective. Jesus was called a drunkard, a wine bibber, and a friend of sinners; but this would have had zero effect on His heart. Jesus had a God-image: I am Jesus, God's Son, and He is well pleased with me. With a God-image that strong, I can tell you, without reservation, those lies had no effect on Jesus. This was probably another point of frustration for His enemies. No verbal attack had any effect on Jesus and we can be just like Him once we have settled in our hearts God's image of us.

God called Jesus His Beloved Son before He had done any earthly ministry. *"And suddenly a voice came from heaven, saying, "This is My beloved Son, in Whom I am well pleased"* (Matthew 3:17). God's love of Jesus was not tied in any way to His performance. This is proof that God's love for you is not tied to your actions. God is pleased with you regardless of any actions. God's declaration over Jesus is evidence of His eternal, unconditional love which is outside of all our actions.

The genuine love of God was the huge motivating factor which enabled Jesus to fulfill His difficult mission. This same knowledge of God's love will be a key to holding onto the vision that God gives you for your future. There may be some difficult times in which you may doubt the grandness of what God has shown you will come to pass. However, in those times it is the realization that a God who loves you enough to show you the future will love you enough to complete it. *"Being confident of this very thing, that He who has begun a good work in you will complete it until the day of Jesus Christ"* (Philippians 1:6).

Why is my freedom irresistible to others?

I believe this understanding of God's love is the reason for another phenomenon that surrounded Jesus. Why did sinners like being around Him? Since we know Jesus is God, and God is Holy, how could this be? Jesus's understanding of His complete acceptance allowed Him to accept others apart from their sins. I believe most of us have not cleared our hearts completely from lies of conditional acceptance. When an unsaved person is in our presence they, most likely, are picking up on our unspoken condemnation of their actions because we are still judging ourselves on our performance. As we grow in our relationship with God and His unconditional love for us, we should experience more freedom from this unspoken condemnation toward others. The proof will be unbelievers, who are searching for the truth, becoming more comfortable in our presence.

The attractiveness of Jesus caused people to want to change their lives, without Him having to point out their sin. People desired what He had apart from being told what they must <u>do</u> or <u>not do</u> to get it. The acceptance that Jesus offered was born out of His love for His creations. He genuinely wanted to be near them. He did not care where they were. He was not taking, but giving. We must be vigilant in our spiritual journey to not allow self-centered motives to slip back into our lives. As we diligently keep our focus on others, we can have the same magnetic attraction to unbelievers who are looking for the truth.

Chapter 13

How Is Comparison a Strategy of War?

How does Satan use comparison to shift our standard?

Earlier I explained the incredible amount of uniqueness in each person on earth. The ultimate lesson learned was that, not only has God made every single person distinctly different, that difference is on purpose. We also saw that our uniqueness is the key to unlock our spiritual destiny. Therefore, Satan will target this area. We have talked briefly about his attempts to destroy our imagination at a young age, but a strategy effective at any age is comparison. The reason comparison is so effective in derailing your future is that it easily takes you off the rails of your true standard: God loves me. All other standards are unstable. Remember the analogy of standing in the rocking chair.

Comparison itself is not evil. I can observe someone who is diligent, admire that quality, and even seek to emulate it in my own life. Comparison is only evil when we use it for the purpose of making judgments to determine value. Examples of this would be: they are more diligent than I, therefore, I am lazy; or I am thin, therefore, this makes me more valuable because they are fat and I am not.

There is absolutely no positive outcome from this type of comparison. I can see at least three negative scenarios. First, you think you are better than the other person and can be filled with pride, which is the same sin as the devil. Second, you think you are inferior to the other person, and chose to stop pursuing excellence in that area with the rationale being: why do it if someone else can do it so much better? Or third, you think you are inferior therefore, you choose to prove your worth through your performance. The comparison trap is a one hundred percent effective snare of the devil. If you step in it, you're caught.

Once you compare yourself to someone else for valuation, you are no longer deriving your worth from God's love. You are now accessing your worth based upon a continuously changing standard. Who will you compare yourself to next and what will be the nature of that comparison? Are they taller, do they dress better, do they make better grades, are they a better teacher, are they funnier than you, do they make more money, etc.? The only way to accept and love who you are is to know that you are already loved and accepted by God (Ephesians 1:6).

Once you step off of the unconditional acceptance of God as the foundation of self-worth, what is to be the basis of your value? I realize this sounds horrible, but this is where many of us actually live. Many people, after being born again, only grow in a head knowledge of God's love for them. Their hearts are unable to grasp the unconditional acceptance they have through Jesus. So, they continue going through their Christian life assessing themselves compared to everyone else. You will be shocked when you discover how often comparison is a part of your everyday thought process.

Underneath comparing is the need for self-worth.

"For we dare not class ourselves or compare ourselves with those who commend themselves. But they, measuring themselves by themselves, and comparing themselves among themselves, are not wise" (2 Corinthians 10:12). This verse clearly points out the underlining problem with comparison. It is the measuring of one against another that is unwise. Notice that the people doing the comparing are endeavoring to validate themselves in order to commend themselves. This verse points out that underneath comparison is our need for self-worth. We have clearly seen that our worth must come from the love God has for us. As God's love becomes relevant in our hearts, the need that fuels the comparison is stripped away. In this place of freedom, you are not struggling to be happy for someone else's blessing. With your own worth established, there is no need for another measure. You are free to love others without comparing.

How do I discern comparison, envy, and selfishness?

Comparison is so ingrained in our subconscious that it can be almost impossible to be happy for the blessing of others without comparing it to our own situation.

How would you act if someone you knew received a lot of money unexpectedly? Be honest with yourself about your true feelings. Hopefully, you could be truly happy for their blessing. Admittedly though, if we do not diligently guard our hearts, conflicting thoughts may harass us. A subtle shift after the initial happiness could be followed by the thought, what about my blessing, God? Comparison is so ingrained in our subconscious that it can be almost impossible to be happy for the blessing of others without comparing it to our own situation.

How do we fight these feelings and where are they coming from? *"For where envy and self-seeking exist, confusion and every evil thing are there"* (James 3:16). <u>Envy</u> is defined as: the painful awareness of an advantage possessed by another with the desire to possess that advantage. Our friend's sudden blessing has exposed envy in our hearts. Most of us don't think we envy, but if your friend won ten million dollars, how would you feel? What if they are not as diligent and hard working as you think you are, then how would you feel? Now we are discovering the true condition of our heart, not what we think it is. The truth that sets us free is not always pleasant, yet it is necessary in order for us to walk out of our deceptions.

It is impossible to envy without having compared first.

The key to stopping these thoughts is to realize that it is impossible to envy without having compared first. Comparison is the gasoline for envy. If you do not put gas in the car, then the car is unable to go anywhere. Comparison is the lie you can cast down, envy is the lie planted in your heart. It is a lot easier to stop comparison before it goes into the tank of your heart than to drain the tank after it is already there. Stopping comparison is a key to ending many self-centered thoughts. Someone who re-directs their focus toward others, rather than self, is becoming a clearer channel of God's revelation to set people free.

It pains me to say this, but those negative feelings about the unexpected blessing in your friend's life, are coming from the root of selfishness. In James 3:16 <u>self-seeking</u> is defined as: looking out for your own interest, or basically, selfishness. If we are self-focused our joy for our friend will be fleeting. It is all about where, by an act of our free will, we chose to direct our attention. Our attention can be directed outward toward others, or inward toward ourselves. A parable that Jesus tells in Mathew 20:1-15 is great for highlighting this inward focus and the underlying feelings that it brings up in our relationship with God.

In summary, the story is about a vineyard owner who hired workers in the morning and agreed to pay them a full day's wage. All through the day he continued to hire more workers and agreed to settle their wages at the end of the day. That evening he first paid the last workers who had only worked one hour, giving them a full day's wages. When the first workers came, they received their agreed upon daily wage. Those who were first hired complained about this not being fair. Here is the owner's response: *"Friend, I am doing you no wrong. Did you not agree with me for a denarius? Take what is yours and go your way. I wish to give to this last man the same as to you. Is it not lawful for me to do what I wish with my own things? Or is your eye evil because I am good?" (Matthew 20:13-15).* What is really happening when someone else comes into something nice and you envy them? I want to focus on the phrase *"Or is your eye evil because I am good?"* The word <u>evil</u> means: hurtful in effect or influence. What you are really saying is that God doesn't know what He is doing, so you have set yourself up as their judge. Your perception of what the other person deserves has become evil or hurtful toward them. You are literally questioning the goodness of God.

As we recognize our strongholds and resist these old familiar paths of deception, our own hearts become beacons of light guiding the way for others. Psalms 119:105 says it this way, *"Your word is a lamp to my feet and a light to my path."* Without our agreement with the lies, God is able to fully illuminate the plans He has for our future. When something good happens to someone else, we are genuinely able to praise God with them, from our heart, not having to fake our happiness for them.

When something great happens to you, who do you want to tell first? These are the freest people you know.

I am about to reveal to you the freest people you know. When something great happens to you, who do you want to tell first? These are the freest people you know. How can I be so sure? Because, your first impulse is to share your good news with people you are certain will be happy for you. Now think again about who you would want to tell first. I am willing to bet they are very unselfish. You want to be one of those people. You do not want to be the type of person someone would call last, fearing they would not be happy for you.

Once, after teaching this, I had someone from the audience come forward and tell me that she had been parking her new luxury car two blocks from work and walking so that her co-workers would not see it. I cannot imagine what it was like working in a place where everyone exuded that much selfishness. She did not realize she was being enslaved by their self-centeredness. She originally thought she was just being humble. If you find yourself afraid to tell someone good news about yourself, it is probably because their world revolves around them and your news will not make their world better, only worse by comparison. It is a sure sign they are totally self-absorbed.

If confusion and every evil thing are in the presence of envy and self-seeking (James 3:16), then what are the opposites of these two evils? We should be determined to have the opposites of these in our hearts. The opposite of envying someone would be to celebrate who they are apart from how it relates to you. The opposite of self-seeking would be to look out for the interests of others. Here then is the positive side of what James 3:16 teaches us. Where there is celebrating others and unselfishness, there is clarity and every good work. I just described God's heart to you and how He would like people to relate to one another. This is His model for how His church is to relationally stand out from the rest of the world. *"By this all will know that you are my disciples, if you have love for one another"* (John 13:35). Notice that this relationship model brings clarity of purpose, the opposite of confusion. Revelation is a natural byproduct of a mind that is uncluttered with thoughts of comparison.

There is not a selfish thought in the heart of God, and as we focus on what He focuses on, selfishness fades away.

The opposite of focusing on ourselves is to focus on others. *"And let us consider one another in order to stir up love and good works"* (Hebrews 10:24). The word consider means: to observe fully. Stir up means: to provoke or incite. So we are to intently look at fellow Christians in order to provoke them into love and good works. When we are following this relational model, we are acting in the very character of God. 1 Corinthians 13:5 says, *"Love does not seek its own."* There is not a selfish thought in the heart of God and, as we focus on what He focuses on, selfishness fades away. The simple solution to destroying envy and selfishness is to direct our thoughts outward to encourage and build up others.

The problem of selfishness is not new to our current society. It was going strong in one of the leading first century churches. Paul, an older apostle praises a younger leader, Timothy, for <u>not</u> being like everyone else. *"For I have <u>no one</u> like-minded, who will sincerely care for your state. For <u>all seek their own</u> not the things which are of Christ Jesus" (Philippians 2:20-21).*

As a leader, you cannot expect someone you are leading to be less self-centered than you are.

The strongest model for leadership is that of a servant leader. This is someone who puts the needs of others above their own. Jesus is our best example of this type of servant leadership. If, however, selfishness gets in the heart of the leader the roles are easily reversed. It becomes all about what my people can do for me. We need to test our motives by asking a critical question: am I doing it for them, or am I doing it for me? Selfishness in leadership has a cascading effect as it flows toward those influenced by the leader. As a leader, you cannot expect someone you are leading to be less self-centered than you are.

The Pharisees and Sadducees were the religious leaders during the time of Jesus's ministry. They had made the mistake of stepping out of their servant leadership role to the people, and had become self-centered in their hearts. It says in Matthew 27:18 that Pilate, the Roman governor, knew these leaders had handed Jesus over to him to be killed because of envy. Jesus was drawing large crowds, He was performing miracles, and healing many people. If their hearts had been in alignment with God's heart, they would have celebrated

Jesus's ministry. However, they were ensnared by Satan's trap of comparison, and the resulting envy caused them to hate Jesus. Envy is one step away from murder. We want to fight the comparison that fuels this monster. These leaders compared, they envied, and they committed murder.

What happened to the very first brothers on the earth, Cain and Abel? What was the motive behind Cain's murder of his brother, Abel? It was envy. Abel had a relationship with God and his offering was accepted because he gave it from a right heart. God rejected Cain's offering because his motive for giving was not right. Cain envied Abel's relationship with God and he murdered his own brother because of it. Cain compared, he envied, and he committed murder.

What about the two sisters, Rachel and Leah, in Genesis 29-30? Leah got in bed with Jacob, her sister Rachel's fiancée, on their wedding night. I don't believe there is a more selfish story in the entire Bible. What was driving this hideous action? Leah compared her lack of a husband to Rachel and Jacob's true love. Leah envied Rachel, her younger sister, who she felt was more beautiful and was now getting married before her. The pattern is the same as before. She compared, she envied, and she committed a shocking sin whose foundation was self-seeking. She had permanently maimed her sister's marriage and would continue to do so for the rest of their lives.

The real irony of this story is that once Leah was in the marriage, which she got into by comparison and envy, she then tricks Rachel into stepping into the same trap of comparison. Although Jacob was deceived into marrying Leah first, he did marry Rachel soon after and now has two wives that are sisters. Leah, realizing that she is not loved, gets into a comparison war with Rachel over the number of children they are able to have for their husband. Rachel goes right along with the comparison trap that the devil has set through her sister, Leah.

Here is the double irony: Rachel could have won a comparison war without even trying because she had something that Leah would never have. Rachel had the unconditional true love of Jacob, her husband, who had worked to earn her hand in marriage for seven years. In like manner, we are comparing ourselves to others when we have the unconditional love of God. All Rachel had to do was say, "But, he loves me." All we have to do to resist comparison is to boldly declare, "I will not compare, because God loves me." The mental process that Leah had to go through to rationalize this kind of sin is a topic we will be covering later under the heading of self-justification in Chapter 15.

How do I resist comparison in ministry?

Just as Rachel and Leah compared natural offspring; similarly, ministers compare spiritual offspring.

I want to highlight comparison in Christian ministry, as it seems to be especially devilish in nature. Even while writing this book I am being bombarded with lies that are telling me: you are not doing enough compared to _____; you should be speaking more; or so and so is going everywhere, no one even knows who you are. It is as if once you have decided to obey God's plan for your destiny, you are under a constant barrage of lies. The bombardment is usually laced with comparison everywhere. If two pastors meet, it is very likely that one will have to ask the other about how many they are running. Translated this means: I need to know how many attend your church so I can compare it to mine.

Just as Rachel and Leah compared natural offspring; similarly, ministers compare spiritual offspring. The spiritual children reproduced from these types of fathers and mothers will only reproduce after their own kind. If we, as Christians, take the bait of comparison into our Christian DNA then whole generations are raised without the understanding of the intimacy needed to reproduce a genuine disciple of Christ. Comparison replaces the foundation of the love of God as commanded in Deuteronomy 6:5, *"You shall love the Lord your God with all your heart, with all your soul, and with all your strength."* This new foundation of comparison instantaneously marginalizes the love of God. Comparison, especially in ministry, has to be resisted the same as stealing or adultery; the repercussions are just as severe.

While in Bible college I watched with disappointment as comparison was used to stop the heart of God from flowing out of my fellow students. We were required to teach short messages in front of our peers. I could see despair in the eyes of students as they compared themselves to more dynamic speakers. It was as if 1 Samuel 16:7 did not apply. *"…For the Lord does not see as man sees; for man looks at the outward appearance, but the Lord looks at the heart."* I would love to have seen the motivation of our hearts behind our messages from God's perspective.

In genuine God-directed ministry, the focus is always on the people we are serving; comparison is Satan's attempt to shift the focus to our performance. I doubt if Jesus was thinking about His delivery while teaching the Sermon on the Mount, or how His profile looked as He healed a blind man. If you will commit yourself to be vigilant to fight these thoughts, the acquired habit will prove life changing. If you are asked to teach, then only teach what God has shown you to share with those listening. Here is the point that kills comparison in ministry. God told you what to say. It is not important because you are saying it; it is important because the God who created heaven and earth asked you to share it. It does not matter the extent to which we are harassed with comparison, we must obey God.

God can reveal anything to any person to share with whomever He desires. Thank God that He trusts us enough in our relationship with Him to have us share with someone else. We must be obedient and fight through the comparison. If God had wanted someone else to share, He would have asked them. Our sharing is how the God of love communicates to the objects of His affection. Comparison is attempting to turn our focus inward. Be obedient, push through the lies of comparison, and let God use you. Only God knows why He picked you for a particular assignment. Since He is God, it must have been a wise decision.

What does an unchained mind look like?

A mind that avoids the comparison trap is free to explore the original creative ideas that God breathes into it, without measuring those ideas against the ideas of others. Your childlike imagination flourishes best in the realm of unrestricted possibility. This is where the relationship with God is the most fun and exciting. God will show you great big possibilities. Once you have become childlike in your pursuit of Him, you begin to believe that if your loving heavenly Father showed it to you then, of course, He will bring it to pass. The co-creation of your future is near to God's heart.

Most of the time, God is unable to give someone their future because they believe they are incapable of accomplishing it.

From Jeremiah 29:11 we saw that God desires to give you a future and a hope. Most of the time, God is unable to give someone their future because they believe they are incapable of accomplishing it. This self-devaluation comes through comparison, never from the heart of God. God believes all things and hopes all things about you and your future. From our perspective, God's future plans must always seem impossible or they would not require faith on our part. Hebrews 11:6 says that without faith it is impossible to please God. When our child-like faith matches with God's heart to give us a future, we have become one with God in heart and in purpose. This is the very place of agreement we spoke of earlier where we are unstoppable; the place where God can be Himself. The place where a loving, creative Visionary is unhindered by the only thing that has ever slowed Him down: our unbelief. This is where David's heart was when he killed Goliath.

I cannot overemphasize the positive benefits that will fill your life once you see yourself loved by God, apart from the need to compare yourself to anyone.

A turning point for me in the mental fight against comparison was when I realized just how insane it really was. Since God had shown me that everyone on earth was unique on purpose, that meant there was no one to compare myself with. God had shown me that all outcomes of comparison are negative. Therefore, since there is no positive outcome from comparing, the wisdom of God is to not allow comparison in our hearts.

Part of taking every thought captive, mentioned in 2 Corinthians 10:5, must be to deny yourself the right to compare. If you will resist comparison, as you would any other sin, you will find that it will flee from you. For most of us, however, no one has ever explained this foolish trap. I cannot overemphasize the positive benefits that will fill your life once you see yourself loved by God, apart from the need to compare yourself to anyone. While on earth Jesus served as our perfect example of what is possible without the limiting restriction of comparison. He was bold, confident, joyful, content, obedient, faithful, gentle, forgiving, and the list could go on. Comparison's goal it to prevent you from achieving freedom in your life.

Chapter 14

Why Am I Being Minimalized?

What are the strategies to put me down?

A <u>minimalist</u> is: someone who favors restricting the functions of an organization or the achievement of a set of goals to a minimum. To accurately describe Satan's plans against you, I will be creating a new word <u>minimalization</u>. I define it as follows: the exertion of outside forces upon a group or individual for the purpose of minimalizing their effectiveness or influence. Satan's objective for your life is to minimalize the influence you will have for good. As we have observed, the most effective way for him to do that is to distort your understanding of the knowledge of God. The specific strategy of deception, attempting to make you feel less significant than you actually are, is what I call <u>minimalization</u>.

A tactic used for minimalizing you is the re-direction of your focus from others toward yourself (selfishness). Initially, this involves shifting from relationship to performance which is a powerful tool in minimalizing your impact. Selfishness will make you susceptible to comparison and envy. Selfishness will redirect your standard from a one-of-a-kind child of God to a distorted self-image that derives its worth based on comparison to others.

As we have clearly seen, you are a unique creation. As a child of God you are completely accepted by God through Jesus's work on the cross. You are indwelt with the power of the Holy Spirit. None of these truths hinge in the least bit on your ability to perform. The story of Moses at the burning bush is a perfect example of someone who had fallen prey to this strategy of minimalization. Moses's first words after God's call to active duty were, *"Who am **I** that **I** should go to Pharaoh, and that **I** should bring the children of Israel out of Egypt?"* *(Exodus 3:11).*

The devil had established a self-image in Moses which was quite different from God's image of Moses. The devil had effectively killed Moses's hope. If you add to this a long passing of time (in Moses's case, forty years) it is easy to see how anyone could have lost hope. It is crucial, in an extended time of waiting, to not take our eyes off of God and His abilities. If God has shown us details concerning our future, why would He not bring it to pass? Remember, if God has a plan, He never changes His mind.

Performance based acceptance is the weak foundation that many build their self-image upon. The world's system of performance based acceptance is not how God's kingdom operates. The Kingdom of God operates on the unmerited love of God, which is given freely without expectation of return. The world that we live in operates under the philosophy that if you scratch my back, I will scratch your back. If Satan can get us to believe that our destiny is based solely on our abilities to bring it to pass, then any moment of weakness on our part will effectively destroy hope for our future.

How does my value make me a target?

God set the value on us before we ever did anything.

Earlier I spoke about your worth. I explained that it was not based on a self-estimation of value, but is based on what someone else was willing to pay. Since Jesus Christ's life was paid to redeem you out of sin and back into a covenant relationship with God, you are worth what was paid for you. You are worth the life of Jesus Christ. I know I am repeating myself here, but I believe it is necessary because the shame of our sins will drive us away from this fact. Therefore, it is important to reiterate this essential truth. Our performance has nothing to do with our worth. *"But God demonstrates His own love toward us, in that while we were still sinners, Christ died for us" (Romans 5:8).* God set the value on us before we ever did anything. He also said Jesus was His beloved Son in whom He was well pleased, prior to Jesus ever doing any ministry. The bottom line is: your worth is immeasurable. You are valuable to God regardless of your performance. This is true whether you realize it or not.

Satan is fully aware of the value God has placed on us, even if we are not. Picture envy beyond all comprehension; the extreme envy that led the people we spoke of earlier to murder. That envy was inspired or stirred up in those individuals by Satan. The devil deeply envies the special place that we occupy in God's heart. Just like Cain envied Abel, Leah envied Rachel, and the Pharisees envied Jesus; Satan envies the position of prominence that we have in our relationship with God. It is a higher position than he ever held, even before he was thrown out of heaven. He is motivated by this envy which provokes him to undermine your attainment of your destiny.

Why is encouragement so influential?

Have you ever had someone give you a genuine, heartfelt compliment, which seemed to stay with you for a long time? I have heard of elementary school teachers who can remember compliments from their students' parents from 20 years ago. The reason a simple word could have such long lasting impact is that there is a shortage of kind, encouraging, and uplifting words. When someone takes the time to speak an encouraging word into your life, it can change everything; it is like wind in your sails. Most of us receive very little encouragement. When we do receive encouraging words, they are remarkably influential.

Your ability to change the lives of others through encouragement, is one of the main reasons the devil wants your effectiveness minimalized.

Giving encouragement can be just as rewarding. *"A man has joy by the answer of his mouth, and a word spoken in due season, how good it is!" (Proverbs 15:23).* This is why the gift of prophecy is so effective when used correctly. 1 Corinthians 14:3 explains the purpose of prophecy, *"But he who prophesies speaks edification and exhortation and comfort to men."* When you prophesy to someone you are, by the power of God's Spirit, encouraging them by verbally communicating God's heart toward them.

Your ability to change the lives of others through encouragement is one of the main reasons Satan wants your effectiveness minimalized. This action of edifying and uplifting encourages people to continue forward in the plans that God has for their life. It is one of the most effective things that you can do in God's Kingdom. It has the power to give people the strength to go on, even if outwardly things are not going well. If you are tuned into God's voice, you will find yourself encouraging others at the exact moment they need it the most. Just when they are about to give up, God will send you to encourage them to stay the course.

This edifying of others to move into their destiny is spoken of in Revelation 19:10 "... *For the testimony of Jesus is the spirit of prophecy.*" The word testimony used here means: evidence. This means the evidence that Jesus is at work is that edification, exhortation, and comfort will be coming forth. As I am writing I feel the need to edify others more. I think all of us can easily slip back into our own self-centered world and forget there is such a profound need for encouragement in the lives of everyone.

As we look at Hebrews 10:24 again, "*Let us consider one another in order to stir up love and good works,*" we can see that purposefully encouraging others is at the very heart of God. I would like to encourage you to focus on someone as you go about your daily activities. You will be amazed, when you are able to speak to them, how quickly you may enter into prophecy. You might begin to speak things about them that you could not have known other than by the Spirit of God. This is the doorway to the prophetic and the very heart of Jesus. Jesus's thoughts dwell on the destiny of His bride. We are what He is thinking about. "*Lord, our God, no one can compare with You. Such wonderful works and miracles, are all found with You! And You think of us all the time, Thinking of us all the time With Your countless expressions of love Far exceeding our expectations!*" *(Psalms 40:5 TPT)*. If we enter into thinking about who

Jesus cares about, then we will not have to work to understand the spiritual gift of prophecy; we will be in the middle of it.

How big is my box?

How can we be living so far below the unlimited potential of the Holy Spirit of God who lives in us?

Remember the funny story I told earlier about when I was so proud of myself because I was thinking outside of the box? God's response was profound to say the least. He said, "There is no box." This brings up a very humbling question. How can we be living so far below the unlimited potential of the Holy Spirit of God who lives in us? I believe it is because Satan's strategies targeted at minimalizing us have, for the most part, been effective. That is why I am taking the time to emphasize this particular tactic of his warfare. Anytime something hidden in darkness is brought to the light of truth, it loses the power it possesses through concealment. Now that you know an enemy is likely to attack you with minimalizing lies, you will recognize them when they come.

This tactic of minimalization is designed to destroy your belief in your potential. Our expectations of our influence should be measured by God's abilities and not our own. If our self-image is derived from our abilities, and not God's abilities, then our estimate of our influence will be far below God's image of our potential. Jesus's measure of our potential is stated in John 14:12, *"Most assuredly, I say to you, he who believes in Me, the works that I do he will do also; and greater works than these he will do, because I go to My Father. And whatever you ask in My name, that I will do, that the Father may be glorified in the Son. If you ask anything in My name, I will do it."* Jesus was starting us where He left off, but believed we would do greater than what He had done; only limited by what we were willing to ask for. It sounds like Jesus doesn't believe there is a box.

What do you see when you look in the mirror? You see yourself based on what you perceive to be true about how you look. Do you realize that the appearance of who you see in the mirror might not actually be the truth of what you look like? The discrepancy originates in the distortion of your self-image. As we refer back to **Diagram C**, God's eye of love on the left has completely clear vision, while our own eyes can become evil or clouded as they are exposed to Satan's deceptions of who he would like us to think we are.

When you are looking in the mirror, God is also looking at that image. He sees someone uniquely made, who He loves, and who He thinks is absolutely beautiful. If this is not what you see when you look in the mirror, you are deceived. That seems a bit harsh, but it is true. Your image of your physical appearance can be distorted by personal insults. If someone once told you that your ears are too big, and you believed them, then when you look in the mirror you see someone with big ears. In exactly the same way your appearance is attacked by lies, your potential is also a target for lies.

Here is a good example. If someone has told you that you are not smart enough to be a doctor and you believed them, this will produce a self-image of someone who believes they are not intelligent. Here is the irony: if you aren't smart enough to be a doctor, you would have never heard the lie in the first place. Satan does not attempt to sabotage a plan that he doesn't believe will be successful. This lie is probably a good indication you need to start looking for scrubs.

God is not, nor will He ever be, in the limiting business.

There is no upper limit that God has placed on you. Any limit you have set, any box that you have placed around your abilities, was set by you, not God. Now I am hearing you say, but _____, but _____. Every "but" that you have ever said about what cannot be done, is an indication that you are self-focused and not God-focused. God's potential is unlimited. If you could only see His potential in you, you would not have a "but" for anything that God had shown you. If you saw yourself clearly, like God does, you would see Christ's potential in you. For you to say, "I can't", would be equivalent to saying, "God can't".

This is the same understanding which had permeated the heart of David as a young shepherd. He had come to the place where he could not see himself separate from God. He was one with God in heart and purpose. This mentality infected over three hundred of his men, and they became known as <u>David's mighty men</u>. God had demonstrated, through David's example, that the only limit they really had was the limit they had placed on God's power in them. With this understanding, read about their exploits in 2 Samuel 23:8-21.

God is not, nor will He ever be, in the limiting business. I am told that the universe is still expanding since the moment He created it. The concept of <u>the box</u> could not have been conceived by God. If God believes it and says it, then it is so. How is that for unlimited? And God's Holy Spirit lives in those who believe in Him. This is the same Spirit Who hung the galaxies in place.

Jesus spoke of our potential again in Mark 11:23, *"For assuredly, I say to you, whoever says to this mountain, 'Be removed and be cast into the sea,' and does not doubt in his heart, but believes that those things he says will be done, he will have whatever he says."* Fears of all kinds push against any endeavor that might allow us to free others. As a very practical way to resist these fears, I would encourage you to always be facing them. Preferably, whatever you do should be an activity that exposes lies about your self-image. Lies such as you are going to look stupid and what will people think of you, are usually refuted best in front of an audience. The refusal to give in to those doubts and fears, before and during your presentation, is one of the fastest ways to expose them for the lies they really are. This is taking an offensive approach, rather than laying back in a defensive position.

Who has pushed through?

Have you ever heard of George Washington Carver?[A] He was born a slave in 1864 and grew up in the southern part of the United States. Mr. Carver became a follower of Jesus at an early age. He went on to become a distinguished agricultural scientist. One of his significant achievements was discovering the many uses of the peanut. One of the amazing things about Mr. Carver was that he had to overcome overwhelming obstacles all around him. He was a black man in the south who went to college and became a world renowned scientist during times of strong racial prejudice against black people. He was even kidnapped as a child with the intent to sell him as a slave.

Mr. Carver was able to think outside of <u>the box</u> which his world had put him in because he believed that God had a purpose for his life. He believed God cared about the people his research would help and God would show him what was necessary to create many new uses for agricultural products. He helped to save and create whole new industries, despite his apparent limitations. Mr. Carver refused to believe the lies of minimalization that the enemy had surrounded him with. He saw himself in God where there were no limits. Because of his faith, God revealed to him many creative ideas. He was a man who had learned to live outside of <u>the box</u> of self-image that Satan had tried to put him in.

The greatest King of Israel, King David, had to overcome a giant relational heartache as a young man. Apparently neither David's father, Jesse, nor his brothers thought very much of David as a youth. When Samuel came to anoint one of Jesse's sons to be king of Israel, Jesse did not even consider his son David worthy of being called to dinner with his brothers. Later, when David was taking food to his brothers on the battlefront, they treated him with contempt.

How does someone with such little positive relational support grow up to receive the highest compliment that God has ever given a man? God said of David *"…the Lord has sought Him a man after His own heart…" (1 Samuel 13:14)*. David refused to believe the lies of minimalization that surrounded him, even those inflicted by his own family. David spent so much time alone as a young shepherd, I believe his time with God became more real to him than the lies. David began to imagine himself as brave and fearless. He began to act on that imagination by killing a lion and a bear as a young man.

I spoke earlier of Gideon. Gideon must have imagined himself as a brave leader or he could not have believed what God was telling Him. Joseph, the son of Jacob, also had to keep his eyes on his dreams as a young man, rather than look at the betrayal of his brothers that sold him into slavery. Joseph had to look past the betrayal of his Egyptian master's wife. He had to look past being forgotten in prison.

Joseph was able to do this because he believed God had a plan for his life. You, too, have to believe God has a destiny for you, that He created you uniquely for a reason. There is a practical way to do this.

How much do I imagine?

God imagines everything before He brings it into existence and you are made in His image.

How much time do you spend dreaming about your future? How much time do you spend imagining what it will be like when you are living in the full potential of what God desires for your life? At a young age Satan will seek to destroy your imagination. You are created in the image of your Creator, God. God imagines everything before He brings it into existence and you are made in His image. If you can get a firm picture in your heart about anything and believe it is possible, then it will come to pass. *"As a man thinks in his heart so is he"* (Proverbs 23:7).

The lies to attack creative imagination are aggressive and ugly. Here are just a few: you're arrogant, you're prideful, you are making this all about you, that has not been done before, you are crazy, you are going to make a fool out of yourself, that is more than ____ has ever done and he is famous, those are just vain imaginations, you're not smart enough, you're too old, you're too young, you're weird, you're a freak, nobody thinks like that. I am not sure this list even has an end! Rejecting these lies before they get in your heart is crucial to preventing the derailment of your destiny.

There will come a point in your life, if you believe God and will not quit, that all the naysayers will be silenced.

Daydream, imagine, and become the little child who does not know the difference between reality and what his heart sees. Because what you really see, by the power of God's Spirit, becomes reality. Nobody laughed at David after he cut off the head of the giant, Goliath. There will come a point in your life, if you believe God and will not quit, that all the naysayers will be silenced. Believe God has a plan for you, ask Him to show you, and daydream about it until it comes to pass. Because, if He showed you, it will come to pass! Heaven and earth may fail, but God's special word to you, His one-of-a-kind child, will stand forever. Don't let a lie be the reason you let go of God's destiny for your life.

Your imagination should be big, because your God is big.

I have always spent a lot of time imagining the future. I was proud of myself one day because I could imagine God using me to do great things. God reminded me of Ephesians 3:20-21, *"Now to Him who is able to do exceedingly, abundantly <u>above all that we ask or think</u>, according to the power that works in us, to Him be glory in the church by Christ Jesus to all generations, forever and ever. Amen."* I believe God was showing me, through His word, that if I could think it, it was too small. His word says He will do above all that we can ask or think.

God also showed me the lack of effort needed to imagine, which brings up an interesting question. Does it take any more effort on our part to believe for something big than it does to believe for something small? The answer is simply no. We may as well believe that God can use us mightily. There is no effort in visualizing the future; in fact, as children we did it naturally. As adults it is usually discouraged with phrases like, "get to work" or "stop day dreaming."

God is usually not the one urging you to get to work. We are like our heavenly Father Who first gets a clear picture and then proceeds to create what He has seen. If most of us spent more time on the perceived <u>impractical</u> work of imagining then the actual <u>practical</u> work would go more smoothly.

God creates big, because He imagines big. Don't fall into the trap of only imagining something that you could logically accomplish on your own. You are not on your own; God is always in you. Your imagination should be big, because your God is big. God wants to give you your future through a vision that He places in your heart. Don't forget Jeremiah 29:11, *"For I know the thoughts and plans that I think toward you, says the Lord, thoughts of peace and not of evil, to give you a future and a hope."* God wants you to co-create with Him to bring His kingdom of truth to all of the earth.

God wants us to think big like He does. God wants to use us to bring Jesus's inheritance to Him. *"Ask of Me, and I will give You the nations for Your inheritance. And the ends of the earth for Your possession"* (Psalms 2:8). Governments are set up by God for the protection of the citizens under their rule. God sees the earth as an organized group of nations. Jesus's inheritance is the people of those nations. Don't be afraid to believe God can use you to influence a nation for Him; that is not too big. It is in complete agreement with His will.

[A] George Washington Carver © John Perry 2011, Publisher Thomas Nelson, Inc.

Section 4
Resist, Don't Assist, Your Enemy

Chapter 15

How Do I Help Satan Nail My Coffin?

Who determines the level of my spiritual freedom?

Who is responsible for how much spiritual freedom you experience in your life? The simple answer is, you are. But, the one thing that ultimately determines how free you are is obedience. Obedience might have a negative connotation because we sometimes think of it as a chore that must be done. When obedience is out of a healthy relationship with a loving heavenly Father it is altogether different from a chore. When you believe that God truly loves you and would only ask you to do something that is in your best interest, then to obey does not bring drudgery but anticipation. To say, *"And we know that all things work together for good to those who love God, to those who are called according to His purpose" (Romans 8:28),* is altogether different from believing it in your heart.

I would like to make this more practical by giving a personal example. I have a naturally aggressive, type A personality. I like to get things done as fast as possible even to the point that a set-back or a challenge actually makes me push harder. It is only recently in my Christian life that I have been able to believe that even an apparent set-back of <u>my</u> schedule could also work out in my best interest. While writing this book there have many things that have gone slower than I would have liked. I am starting to actually believe, on a heart level, that it will work out better than if <u>my</u> timetable had been achieved. Many of us with driven personalities may have never realized this is really a trust issue. To diligently work toward a goal is healthy, but to drive yourself to achieve it is not. The balance is in trusting that God, through His love, is working it out in our best interest.

God desires that we live by faith, so His requests often stretch our understanding.

Trusting in God's love is the only way to have this practical, lasting faith. The solid foundation of God's love is the only foundation that can withstand our own internal resistance to obedience. God's kingdom is not of this world and operates differently than we might think it should, so in our minds there will arise opposition to obedience. One reason we may not desire to obey is because, logically, what God is asking does not make sense to us. God desires that we live by faith, so His requests often stretch our understanding. His desire is that we learn to see through our spiritual understanding and not through our natural eyes. _"For we walk by faith, and not by sight"_ _(2 Corinthians 5:7)._

"If you abide in my word, you are my disciples indeed. And you shall know the truth and the truth shall make you free" _(John 8:31-32)._ The word <u>abide</u> is also translated: to continue. I want to disconnect this verse from the usual connotation of consistent Bible reading, although that is important for spiritual growth. With the understanding of the individual uniqueness of our relationship with God, we can read it this way: if you continue in obedience to the plans I have shown you, you will know Me, and I will set you free to experience the joy of your heart.

Remember the analogy, "You can only kiss one person at a time"? God, through a personal relationship, is talking to you about your individual destiny and not the destiny of everyone as a group. It is your faithful obedience to that <u>kiss</u> which will release you into the highest level of your spiritual freedom.

The only sure way to trust anyone is to get to know them.

Obedience, from a heart of love, is so closely tied to the love relationship that God seldom separates the two. *"But without faith it is impossible to please Him, for he who comes to God must believe that He is, and that He is a rewarder of those who diligently seek Him"* (Hebrews 11:6). Faith is synonymous with trust. God is literally saying that without trusting Him, you cannot please Him. God is also saying we are to move toward Him, believing He will reward our pursuit.

The only sure way to trust anyone is to get to know them. God is welcoming the pursuit of Him in relationship, so that He will be able to do what is His heart's desire - give you a future and a hope. The absolute key to God being able to reward you is your <u>trust based obedience</u>. Duty based obedience (obligation) is weak because it's foundation is built on our strength to perform; trust based obedience is strong because it's foundation is built on the character of God Himself.

The place to receive the most out of any relationship is where there is complete trust between the two parties involved.

Our conditional acceptance mindset causes us to have difficulty interpreting God's heart which is not conditionally based. Because of this, passages like John 15:10 can cause confusion. *"If you keep My commandments you will abide in My love, just as I have kept my Father's commandments and abide in His Love."* God is not saying He will love you <u>if</u> you do what He says. God loves you, because of your worth to Him, irrespective of what you do. This verse is saying that if you continue in trust based obedience you will be in the perfect place to be able to receive the full revelation and experience of God's love.

Disobedience is an indication of a lack of trust. The place to receive the most out of any relationship is where there is complete trust between the two parties involved. If Jesus had chosen to disobey God, God would not have loved Him less. But, He would not have been in the position to receive God's best for Him, which was the joy that had been set before Him. The ultimate plan for Jesus's life was to be united with His bride forever. The fulfillment of that plan required Jesus's obedience. Similarly, the greatest plan for our individual lives requires obedience for it to come to pass. However, we have the free will to choose disobedience, but that choice thwarts the plan from coming to fruition. God's plan is where we will receive the most abundant life possible.

Our relationship with God is actually strengthened by the oppositions we face as we maintain our trust in His plan. Hebrews 5:8, speaking of Jesus says, *"Though He was a Son, yet He learned obedience by the things which He suffered."* The word <u>learned</u> can also be translated: understand. Jesus fully understood obedience by going through the things He suffered. Jesus was tempted by difficulties to disobey. Through His obedience He showed us the way forward to reach our highest calling.

Obedience is the key to spiritual development, and that key is turned by your will whichever way you choose.

Jesus's victory in obedience has given Him the name which is above every name. *"And being found in appearance as a man, He humbled Himself and became <u>obedient</u> to the point of death, even the death of the cross. Therefore God has highly exalted Him and given Him the name which is above every name"* (Philippians 2:8,9). Obedience is the key to spiritual development, and that key is turned by your will whichever way you choose.

How does the Holy Spirit guide my life?

If you are a follower of Jesus Christ, this means the Holy Spirit of God came into your heart the moment you accepted Jesus as your Lord and Savior. The Holy Spirit is also referred to as the Spirit of Truth. Jesus describes Him this way, *"However, when He, <u>the Spirit of truth</u>, has come, He will guide you into all truth; for He will not speak on His own authority, but whatever He hears He will speak; and He will tell you things to come"* (John 16:13). The Holy Spirit, Who is in you, speaks to your heart to guide your spiritual development. One of the ways He does this is by giving you the discernment to recognize the deception of the lies around you. The Holy Spirit might speak to you in an audible voice but usually, it is the voice of your own conscience.

The place you hear the Holy Spirit is where your conscience agrees with the truth and the Holy Spirit is the one presenting the truth.

The Holy Spirit is speaking to you internally. The place you hear the Holy Spirit is where your conscience agrees with the truth and the Holy Spirit is the one presenting the truth. Before the Holy Spirit came to dwell in you, you only had your own heart to discern the truth. In Jeremiah 17:9, we saw that our heart can have tracked or polluted areas of deception. We are predisposed to take these familiar deceptive paths. Once we are indwelt by the Holy Spirit, the truth becomes more clear and we are not as easily deceived. In order to disobey, we must now consciously resist His inner voice of truth.

Obedience without a choice is slavery, not true obedience. God desires your freedom, even if it means you could freely reject the offer of His love. Romans 5:8 says that Christ died for us even before we knew Him. Just because you have the right to reject God's loving guidance, does not mean that there will not be a heavy price to pay when you do. God's awesome plan for your life is at stake. God will not violate your free will. You have the right to choose between the truth and a lie. God loves you with everything that is in His being. He knows that the best plan for your life is to obey Him in every decision that you make. However, He will never force you to obey His will. His desire is that by trusting in His love for you, you will freely choose to obey.

What is self-justification?

Self-justification is the beginning of the end of your spiritual walk with God. It is equivalent to helping Satan nail your coffin! This is how self-justification develops. The Holy Spirit may tell you something like, "You were not very nice to them." What you do next is the most important response influencing your Christian maturity. What can happen is that we come up with a <u>reason</u> for our rudeness such as, "They were rude to me." This is actually an excuse which gives us permission to continue in our sin. This is self-justification. This is the most dangerous response you could choose to make in your Christian life.

Here is a clarification of what just happened. You said, "I am refusing to listen to the Spirit of Truth, given to me for my protection, and I am deciding to listen to a lie." You have begun to lay a pattern of rebellion in your own heart. This decision is a step toward the darkness that surrounds your enemy and away from the light of truth. You have begun to go backwards in your spiritual life, even though God lives on the inside of you.

This is strictly my opinion, but I believe it is better to be openly honest with God in your struggle to obey, than to believe you are justified by your own lies. If the Holy Spirit tells you that you are eating too much, I think it would be better to agree with Him even if you continued in your behavior. I believe this would be better than creating self-deceiving excuses like: everyone eats this much or I deserve a little break, it's not hurting anyone. You might not agree, but I see more danger in believing our own lies than admitting our rebellion.

I have seen the results of the power of self-deception in people's lives that I love and care about. Once the pattern of self-justification is established, it leads to open sin and rebellion against God. Someone who has established the pattern of self-justification will confess Jesus's Lordship and, at the same time, be in open rebellion to His loving commands given for their protection. They are so self-deceived they do not recognize the rebellion in their own heart. This is the ultimate danger of self-justification: self-deception.

"Do you know what is wrong with My church?" "They act like civilians."

One time, without warning, God asked me a question and then immediately answered it. God said, "Do you know what is wrong with My church?" His answer, "They act like civilians." In the military, no soldier would defy his commander-in-chief because of the oath he took to obey. In the same way, for someone to say, "No, Lord," after having made the confession "Jesus is Lord," is an act of open rebellion. However, in many believer's lives there is a sense that they have never enlisted in the Kingdom of God. God may instruct them to do this or not do that, and they will come up with excuses as to why it is not convenient to obey. Although God allows freedom of choice, do not be deceived into thinking His Kingdom is a democracy. It is a

Kingdom and He is the King. To refuse a command is insubordination and open rebellion. If every private quit the army because basic training was hard, where would we be as a nation? Self-justification is nothing more than an excuse to rebel, with the added negative side effect of self-deception. *"The wisdom of the prudent is to understand his way, but the folly of fools is deceit" (Proverbs 14:8).* The wisdom to obey God is rewarded with discernment. The foolishness of rebellion is rewarded with self-deception.

If we are willing to believe our own lies in order to justify our actions, then our ability to perceive the truth has been greatly compromised.

How smart is it to argue with an all-knowing God? When you ask the question framed this way, it highlights how absolutely ridiculous our actions can be. To be in rebellion is one thing, but <u>self-justification births the deception necessary to make us feel at peace with our rebellion</u>. Self-justification is a double edged sword. While it does cut out the pain of our offended conscience, it also cuts out our discernment. If we are willing to believe our own lies in order to justify our actions, then our ability to perceive the truth has been greatly compromised.

Any known disobedience to God can only peacefully co-exist in the life of a believer if they have justified their behavior.

The deceptive path that self-justification starts to wear in the heart is one of embracing a known lie as if it were the truth. Any known disobedience to God can only peacefully co-exist in the life of a believer if they have justified their behavior. This self-justification hardens their heart to hearing the voice of the Holy Spirit, Who they are now purposely trying not to hear. A believer's heart can become so hardened that when they are confronted with known sin in their life, they actually believe that the rules do not apply to them. This, to me, is the most dangerous of all places because the person can no longer be reasoned with on the basis of truth. They have literally created their own new world, with its own rules of right and wrong.

When does God have to get ugly with me?

The only group of people Jesus was harsh with while on the earth was the religious leaders of His day. But why them and no one else? The answer lies in the level of their self-justification. Jesus said to them *"You are those who justify yourselves before men, but God knows your hearts. For what is highly esteemed among men is an abomination in the sight of God" (Luke 16:15).* Because of its length I will not quote Mathew 23 here, but it is one of the most brutal verbal lashings you will ever read. Jesus calls these leaders hypocrites (multiple times), snakes, brood of vipers, and tells them they shall pay for the blood of generations. Since we know God is love, then why is He talking to them like this?

God is love, He can only sound like love, but why is love sounding so unlovely? Jesus loved these leaders, so He must be speaking to them out of His heart of love. Jesus was not being callous as we might be; He was trying to get their attention. He was resorting to this form of tough love because their hearts had become hardened from self-justification. They had reached a point where they could not recognize the truth because of their own self-deception. Jesus was doing this publically trying to shock them into seeing the level of their deception before it was too late.

God is not willing to see anyone perish apart from Him (2 Peter 3:9). The proof that their self-deception had reached epidemic proportions was the extreme manner in which God, Who is love, was speaking. God does not bring shame therefore, this cannot be His motive. But, why did Jesus do this in front of a large crowd? Because they valued men's opinions more than God's, Jesus hoped this public verbal lashing would wake them up to their self-deception. He only did this out of love, and only to deliver them from bondage. In 1 Corinthians 13:5 we read that God is not provoked. But, Love (God) can become exasperated with people who are resisting what is best for them. God was not provoked for His Own sake, but for theirs.

If God has to "yank your chain" then be assured it is a last resort for Him.

If you ever feel God getting ugly with you, I would suggest doing a self-evaluation to see where you began to justify your actions. If God has to "yank your chain" then be assured it is a last resort for Him. He has certainly tried other methods, but your heart is too hard to hear them. Humble yourself quickly, asking Him to expose the level of your deception because, whatever the problem is, it has gone on far too long. *"If we confess our sins, He is faithful and just to forgive us our sins and to cleanse us from all unrighteous"* (I John 1:9). God loves you and wants you free; His correction is always in your best interest. You can trust Him with your feelings of anger and frustration.

God always forgives you immediately, but it might take a while before He reveals where you began to justify your decisions. Be patient and let God show you as He wills. He is kind and gentle enough to only give you what you can handle. His delay in exposing all of your motives is out of His heart of love to protect you from deeper emotional pain. The root cause, leading to the self-justification, can often be a problem which is much more severe than we realize. If God were to show us too much too fast it could bring discouragement instead of the life-giving hope He desires. *"To everything there is a season, a time for every purpose under heaven,"* (Ecclesiastes 3:1) and only God knows the timing!

How does self-justification cause hypocrisy?

The name that Jesus called the religious leaders the most was hypocrite. A hypocrite is someone who claims to believe one thing, yet does the opposite. This is the same hypocrisy we saw in the miser from Proverbs 23:6-7. The miser says he wants you to eat dinner with him, but in his heart he does not want you eating his food. Self-justification causes a division between the heart and the mind of the person believing their own lies. The religious leaders, whom Jesus was confronting, said they followed the laws of God, but they had made up their own laws. Their laws even allowed them to justify not taking care of their aging parents (Mathew 15: 3-9). Jesus says in verse 8, *"These people draw near to Me with their mouth, and honor Me with their lips, but their heart is far from Me."*

The purpose of the lies involved in the process of self-justification is to drive a wedge between your heart and mind.

God's spiritual goal for you is that you be one with Him by His indwelling Holy Spirit, and that can only be accomplished if you are one with Him in the truth. That is because God's Spirit is the Spirit of Truth. *"But the hour is coming, and now is, when the true worshipers will worship the Father in <u>spirit and truth</u>, for the Father is seeking such to worship Him, God is Spirit, and those who* *worship Him must worship in spirit and truth."* (John 4:23-24) The purpose of the lies involved in the process of self-justification is to drive a wedge between your heart and your mind. This leads to a hypocrisy which makes it impossible to worship God as intended. This very effectively keeps you from the abundant life that is yours in God.

Jesus said in John 14:6, *"I am the way, the truth, and the life. No one comes to the Father except through Me."* This can be understood as a progression of deliverance. Jesus is effectively saying, I am the way to get to the truth which will lead you to your real life which is in me. Walking in the truth is absolutely essential to your living in the abundant life that God intends for you.

The lies, which are being whispered to you to justify your actions, are a direct attack against your freedom. Fight to stay honest with yourself about every action and decision that you make. Lies of self-justification are the lies that your natural man wants to believe, which makes them extremely deceptive. You do not have to be overly introspective to be honest with yourself. As long as you are questioning your motives, you will not have a problem. It is when you no longer feel the need to examine yourself that you have opened the door to deception.

How does self-justification cause pride?

What is really happening when God asks us to do something and we come up with a reason not to? Whether we realize it or not, we have just said we are smarter than God. There was once an angel named Lucifer who held a high position in heaven. He did not want to remain in his appointed position; he wanted to exalt himself above God. Therefore, he had to reason that he was smarter than God in order to justify his rebellion. We know him now as Satan. He was cast out of heaven because of his open rebellion. Self-justification causes an extreme pride or, what could be called, haughtiness. This arrogance is what Jesus was trying to deal with when He spoke so harshly to the Scribes and Pharisees.

God will never stop trying to lead someone who is in self-justification, but their believed lies (strongholds) have built walls opposing the truth of His voice.

If you know Christian brothers and sisters who have seemingly abandoned basic Christian morality, understand that this demonic spirit of haughtiness has gotten a grip on their heart. By agreeing with their own lies they have walked away from God's plan for their life. A common characteristic of their lives will be that they find it difficult to hear God's voice of direction. God will never stop trying to lead someone who is in self-justification, but their believed lies (strongholds) have built walls opposing the truth of His voice. God loves them and wants them in the light of His truth where He can guide them again, but they must renounce their rebellion for what it is, apart from any justification.

What is the typical progression of self-justification?

Let's take a look at a practical example of how self-justification can get started in our heart. God could say to me, "Mike, you need to be more compassionate toward your children." To avoid personal responsibility for my actions, I might come up with the defense that they are not helping enough around the house. Whether the excuse is true or not is irrelevant because it has nothing to do with what God asked of me. I just made up an excuse so that I could feel better about not being more compassionate and avoid the requested obedience of the Holy Spirit. Whether I realize it or not, I have just begun a pattern of rebellion.

Next, God might tell me, "Mike, I want you to go to a certain place and teach." After my teaching, God might ask me to stay and pray for the audience, but because my heart was hard about the issue of compassion earlier, I might not have the desire to pray for them. At this point I must come up with another excuse to justify not obeying God's command to pray for the people. I might tell myself that I am very tired and need my rest for tomorrow's session. Once this pattern is established, it creates the hypocrisy that Jesus so loathed in the religious leaders of His day. As leaders they were in positions to set others free, but instead, they were causing people to disdain the very God who loved them because of their hypocritical character.

If you are in any place of spiritual leadership, I pray that you would seriously take this topic to heart. You cannot lead someone to a place you have never been. Always allow the light of God's truth to shine on the dim areas of your heart and do not resist it. Your freedom will be responsible for bringing many more people into their liberty. Because you have clearly seen the dangerous repercussions of any excuses that you might make, be sure to expose all your excuses to the scrutiny of the truth. By doing this you will not only bless your own life abundantly, but the revelation(s) that God gives you in your freedom will deliver many others.

What is the difference between self-justification and self-righteousness?

The word <u>religion</u> has a very positive meaning: the worship of God, or system of actions involved in the worship of God. There is, however, an alternate negative <u>works based religion</u> that is an attempt to deal with our own sins apart from God's grace. This attempted alternate path to gain a right standing with God was seen immediately after man sinned in the Garden of Eden. *"Then the eyes of both of them were opened, and they knew that they were naked; and they sewed fig leaves together and <u>made themselves coverings</u>"* (Genesis 3:7). The first act that was ever performed after mankind sinned was their attempt to deal with sin on their own terms. This obviously was not an acceptable option because God intervened, *"Also for Adam and his wife the Lord God made tunics of skin, <u>and clothed them</u>"* (Genesis 3:21). This pattern of man-centered self-righteousness is so similar to self-justification it is difficult to see any difference at all.

A simple definition of <u>self-righteousness</u> is: to cover oneself. A simple definition of <u>true religion</u> (grace) is: to let oneself be covered by God. True religion is experiencing the grace of God's love. Self-righteousness is taking on the burden of responsibility of dealing with our own sins. This burden of responsibility comes from believing the lie that God has not done enough and it is all up to me. In this man-centered self-righteousness, there is a lack of peace caused by the added responsibility of dealing with our own sins. This lie is life draining and the opposite of the abundant life that Jesus came to bring us.

If you are extremely busy doing things for God and do not have inner peace, check yourself to be sure you have not been deceived in this area. There is nothing at all wrong with being busy but if you feel that you <u>have to</u> be busy, it might be a sign that Satan is trying to steal your peace through the lie of self-righteousness. Don't fall for it; remember, God's love is not based on what you do or don't do.

In self-righteousness we are trying to make our relationship right with God through our own efforts. In self-justification we are trying to believe the relationship is right with God by believing our own lies.

The origin of both self-justification and self-righteousness is found in the relational issue of trust. After man's sin in the garden they could have come to God repentant in their shame, but due to a lack of trust, they chose an alternate route. When we come up with our own excuses for not obeying God, it looks very similar to the sewing of fig leaves that Adam and Eve did to cover themselves. In self-righteousness we are trying to make our relationship right with God through our own efforts. In self-justification we are trying to believe the relationship is right with God by believing our own lies. In self-righteousness the root of our <u>work</u> is the lack of a true understanding of God's love. In self-justification, this same lack of knowledge of God's love leads to the rebellion needed for us to believe our own lies.

Many times you will see self-justification in its most pronounced form when it is intermingled with self-righteousness in religious settings. The hypocrisy of religious activities, without the heart of love that God intended to be motivating them, is what caused such indignation in Jesus toward the religious leaders of His day. A relationship with God, based on the <u>truth</u> of His personality, is the only viable solution to avoiding these alternate paths of self-righteousness and self-justification. It is here we are reminded again that Satan's point of attack is the knowledge of God. Continually walking in the truth of God is the only viable solution to these deceptions, which is my reason for bringing them out into the light of truth. As we expose them, their power is greatly diminished.

Is anyone beyond justifying their actions?

Self-justification is the bait for disobedience, and if I can teach you to recognize the bait, you can avoid being caught on the hook of disobedience.

At this point you might be asking a very legitimate question. Why is he spending so much time on self-justification? The reason is: self-justification is the bait for disobedience. If I can teach you to recognize the bait, you can avoid being caught on the hook of disobedience. My motivation is that by taking such a close look at this tricky deception, you will be able to easily recognize it the next time it comes your way. I want to take a moment here to provide a short list of examples of self-justification from the Bible. This should help all of us realize the universal scope of this problem. God makes it clear in His word that absolutely no one is beyond self-justification.

Job justified his wisdom above God's. *"Would you indeed annul My judgment? Would you condemn Me that you may be justified?"* (Job 40:8). Cain justified killing Abel, his brother (Genesis 4). Abraham justified letting his wife be taken captive by another man (Genesis 12). Jacob justified stealing his brother Esau's blessing (Genesis 27). Leah justified sleeping with her sister's husband on what should have been their wedding night (Genesis 29). Eli justified not dealing with the open immorality of His sons who were temple priests (1 Samuel 2). Elijah justified abandoning his call because of his feelings (1 Kings 19). David (the man after God's own heart) not only justified adultery with Bathsheba, he also justified the murder of Uriah, her husband (2 Samuel 11). The Pharisees justified killing the Son of God (John 11:50).

If you will notice, some of God's closest friends are on this abbreviated list. It is a warning that we must all keep a vigilant watch to avoid taking this attractive alternative to obedience. Psalms 139:23-24 says it best, "*Search me, O God, and know my heart; try me, and know my anxieties; and see if there is any wicked way in me, and lead me in the way everlasting.*"

Why is integrity so powerful?

Earlier we looked at the definition of <u>integrity</u> as: being the same throughout. Probably the most underrated weapon in our spiritual arsenal is the simple weapon of integrity. Just simply being yourself, with no pretense, can be a very strong defense against many of the enemy's tactics. When we pretend to know something we don't know or be someone we are not, we are deceiving ourselves. It's alright not to have the answer, or not to know what to do.

It is important that I not be trapped into thinking I must know it all.

Staying honest with yourself and others is not tantamount to giving up; it is just the true assessment of where you are and nothing more. This honesty is a shield of protection from self-deception. As long as God's word is preached there will be power in it to effect change (Isaiah 55:11). But, there is additional spiritual power when someone is teaching from their heart. Teaching from head knowledge may not produce the desired results the Holy Spirit intends. Satan will attempt to beat you up with what you do not know, but I would encourage you to beat him up with what you do know and further revelation will come. Stay honest with yourself.

It is best if we teach from the inside out. Spiritual power to effect change in ourselves and the lives of others comes from the knowledge of God that has affected our own heart change. I may have a great understanding of one certain subject, but lack revelation on another. It is important that I not be trapped into thinking I must know it all. Believing the lie that I must have all the answers produces an inward desire to fake what I really don't understand. This is the exact same pattern that leads to self-justification, so it is best to stay away from faking anything. Focus on what God has already revealed to you and you will receive more. Never make up something because this can lead to self-deception.

In truth, honesty is the best policy; it not only keeps our hearts honest, but also wins the admiration of others. People will trust you if they know you will only speak the truth, especially if that truth isn't skewed to make you look good. We must be patient with ourselves, God is. This is a learn-as-you-go life, and it takes time. By allowing ourselves the time to change, we will automatically have more patience with others.

This personal integrity opens up a clear channel for God to use us to help others. *"He who believes in Me, as the Scripture has said, out of his heart will flow rivers of living water" (John 7:38).* When the revelation of God, from your heart, is shared with others it carries the life of God in it; this is that <u>living water</u>. People, overall, don't understand how much God loves them. This causes them to reach out for something else to fill that void in their lives. When we have the void in our hearts filled by the true understanding of God, we are able to be a source to direct others to the legitimate longing of their heart. We become like trees bearing fruit from the life-giving water of God. *"He shall be like a tree planted by the rivers of living water, that brings forth its fruit in its season, whose leaf also shall not wither; and whatever he does shall prosper" (Psalm 1:3).*

Chapter 16

How Does Christus Victor Change My Life?

What is the meaning of Christus Victor?

The phrase "Christus Victor"[A] is Latin and means: Christ the Victor. In the early part of the twentieth century it came to be the term used for the classic view of the early church regarding Christ's finished work. A written work by the same name was published in 1931 by Swedish theologian, Dr. Gustaf Aulēn. By comparing three differing views of Christ's sacrificial work of atonement, Dr. Aulēn proves, in my opinion, that the early church held this classic view of Christ's atoning work.

Through Christ's victory, God reconciles mankind with Himself.

This classic, or Christus Victor view, as it came to be known, is very dramatic in nature. In it Christ – Christus Victor – fights against and triumphs over the evil powers of the world, the tyrants under which mankind is in bondage and suffering. Through Christ's victory, God reconciles mankind with Himself. God is pictured as <u>in Christ</u> carrying through a victorious conflict against the powers of evil which are hostile to His will. *"That God was <u>in Christ</u> reconciling the world to Himself, not imputing their trespasses to them, and has committed to us the word of reconciliation" (2 Corinthians 5:19).*

The foundation of this view of Christ's redemptive work is that from the first to the last it is solely a work of God Himself. It means that man is the recipient of the rewards of the work that God performed in Christ, but does not have an active role in bringing them to pass. It is further understood that the reason Christ came down from heaven as a man was because no power, other than God Himself, would be able to accomplish the work that needed to be done. Jesus, the Word of God Himself, entered into the world under the conditions of sin and death to take up the conflict with the powers of evil and carry it through to the decisive victory.

A critical point of the classic view of the early church is that God the Father, God the Son, and God the Holy Spirit were in complete agreement about your rescue. There has never been, nor will there ever be, any disagreement in the Godhead about your worth. They were in agreement before the foundation of the world. *"...just as He [God] chose us in Him [Christ] before the foundation of the world, that we should be holy and without blame before Him in love" (Ephesians 1:4).*

Likewise, the Godhead has always been in agreement about the cost of the rescue. *"All who dwell on the earth will worship him, whose names have not been written in the Book of Life of <u>the Lamb slain from the foundation of the world</u>." (Revelation 13:8)* God loves you unconditionally. He fully knew the cost of restoring to you the opportunity to love Him back. This understanding of the battle fought on your behalf brings a deep heartfelt desire to reciprocate God's love. This was the heart and passion of the early church and the reason for its rapid reproduction across the known world.

Seeing the full gospel as the eternal conflict it is, changes our response to it.

Earlier we called Christ's redemptive work at the cross and subsequent resurrection the <u>rescue mission</u>. We looked closely at Jesus being "The Wedding Savior" sent to save His own wedding. The wedding was believed to have been completely ruined by the devil's planned deception of the bride, but then came our champion, "Christus Victor." 1 John 3:8 was a key verse for our understanding, *"...For this purpose the Son of God was manifested, that He might destroy the works of the devil."*

Christ destroyed Satan's work by being falsely accused and taken into Hell, where He was raised to life victorious over the one who had the power of death - the devil. Colossians 2:15 says of Christ, *"Having disarmed principalities and powers, He made a public spectacle of them, triumphing over them in it."* Having stripped Satan of his power of death, Christ was able to give life freely to all who call on His name. Seeing the full gospel as the eternal conflict it is, changes our response to it. That is the reason I began this book with the explanation of your worth and the need for your rescue. The price for your rescue states, in the most unequivocal terms, the extent of your worth.

How does Christ's victory change my perception?

The self-sacrificial passion with which God's plan was thought out and executed is the only accurate way to fully understand the heart of love that He has for you. Christ came to rescue you at the cost of His own life. He delivered you, so that you would be free to live the abundant life that He had always intended for you to live from the beginning.

Deception was Satan's weapon that caused man to sin against God. It continues to be his only weapon to hinder you from walking into an amazingly abundant life. Understanding the snares of your enemy, the devil, is a critical aspect of avoiding them and continuing to walk in the light of God's love. To walk across a mine-field without knowing the locations of the mines, is to walk in fear. Once you are aware of the locations of the mines, then and only then, can you walk in confidence. To help you see more clearly the methods of Satan's deceptions, and to walk free from the influence of his lies in your life, has been the main objective of this book.

Understanding the love of a Father God and His champion Son, Jesus Christ the Victor, changes the way you value yourself and also the value you place on others. All people are special, one-of-a kind created receivers of the love of God. They are intended to forever live with Him and be one with Him in the closest of relationships. Once this is truly seen at the heart level, you are better equipped to aid in the rescue of others trapped in Satan's deceptions.

Our heart's desire will be that others understand God's love and experience it for themselves. This gospel of love becomes not a have to share message, but a desire to share message. When this happens, God has created in us an open channel for His love to flow toward others. With this understanding of the gospel of love comes the commissioning to be an agent of deliverance on God's behalf.

How does Hosea help us recognize our problem?

In the year 2000, in the middle of the night, this exact thought came to my mind: "Hosea, the book of the prophecy of things to come." I had not received revelation from God this way before, but it was with absolute clarity that I heard those exact words. Hosea was a prophet of Israel whom God asked to marry a prostitute in order to symbolically demonstrate the nation of Israel's unfaithfulness to God. After much adultery, Hosea's wife, Gomer, is sold into slavery. God asks Hosea to continue to love her, so Hosea buys Gomer out of slavery to now be his faithful wife.

I believe God wanted me to see that in the future His church, the bride of Christ, would also be unfaithful and need to be bought again out of slavery. I am bringing this up here because there is a re-occurring theme throughout the book of Hosea. This theme exposes the same target of the devil's deceptions that we looked at in Chapter 1: the knowledge of God.

Here are a few samples of this theme in Hosea. The first also gives us the picture of our marriage to God that we spoke of earlier. *"I will betroth you to Me forever; yes I will betroth you to Me in righteousness and justice, in loving kindness and mercy; I will betroth you to Me in faithfulness, and you shall <u>know the Lord</u>"* (2:19-20). *"... There is no truth or mercy or <u>knowledge of God</u> in the land"* (4:1). *"My people are destroyed for <u>lack of knowledge</u>. Because <u>you have rejected knowledge</u> I also will reject you from being priest for Me..."* (4:6). *"They do not direct their deeds toward turning to their God. For the spirit of harlotry is in their midst, and <u>they do not know the Lord</u>"* (5:4). *"<u>Let us know</u>, let us pursue <u>the knowledge of the Lord</u>..."* (6:3). *"For I desire mercy and not sacrifice, and <u>the knowledge of God</u> more than burnt offerings"* (6:6). In the book of Hosea, God is clearly making the point that the root cause of unfaithfulness to Him is the <u>lack of knowledge</u> of Who He really is.

This lack of understanding of God's desire for relationship has caused some in the church to be unfaithful to the call God has placed on their lives.

We live again in a day where there is a lack of knowledge of the Lord in our land. Even God's church seems to be unclear about His true personality. Many are performing works for God as sacrifices when God clearly says in Hosea 6:6, that He would rather be known than receive sacrifices. This lack of understanding of God's desire for relationship has caused some in the church to be unfaithful to the call God has placed on their lives. They have gone after other lovers (the cares and concerns of this world) because they have never known the depths of the love of God. Now, more than ever, people are needed who will seek after the Lord to know Him in spirit and truth so they can share with others the goodness of God.

God desires to bring His church from a servant relationship into a relationship of intimacy as His bride. *"And it shall be, in that day, says the Lord, that you will call Me 'My Husband', and no longer call Me 'My Master'"* (Hosea 2:16). I believe we are living in the time of Christ's soon return for His bride. Jesus wants us to be in a right relationship with Him before our upcoming marriage in Heaven. We are literally running out of time to get to know Jesus through the indwelling Holy Spirit before He returns. Remember, the main reason we were left on earth was so we could know Him better spiritually before He returns for us physically.

Revelation from God is the incentive for further pursuit of Him.

As we take the time to pursue the knowledge of God's true character, we are assured from scripture that God's desire is to be found by us. *"And you will seek Me and find Me, when you search for Me with all your heart. I will be found by you, says the Lord..."* (Jeremiah 29:13-14). God wants to be found; He has and always will desire relationship.

The only real impediment to knowing God is the lies that are assaulting us about His character and the importance of pursuing Him. Once these lies are confronted head-on, there is an increased ability to receive revelation concerning God's goodness. Revelation from God is the incentive for further pursuit of Him. It is the equivalent of pushing a boulder up a mountain of lies until you reach the top and start down the other side. Once the uphill work is done, the downhill is coasting. I encourage you to agree with the Holy Spirit as He points out the deceptions in your life, and to never resist His voice. God is leading you into an abundant future; a future He has prepared for you and you alone.

How does Christ's victory change my life?

No matter how much we have looked at the evil trickery of Satan's deceptions, I want to leave you with the overwhelming understanding of Christ's Victory. *"Inasmuch then as the children have partaken of flesh and blood, He Himself likewise shared in the same, that through death He might destroy him who had the power or death, that is, the devil, and release those who through the fear of death were all their lifetime subject to bondage"* (Hebrews 2:14-15). This clearly says that we have been freed from death, and the fear that it held over us.

Christ's victory changes your life by giving you an eternal outlook on everything that happens to you.

Although we will physically die, we no longer need ever fear being separated from the love of God. *"For I am persuaded that neither death nor life, nor angels nor principalities nor powers, nor things present nor things to come, nor height nor depth, nor any other created thing, shall be able to separate us from the love of God which is in Christ Jesus our Lord" (John 8:38-39).* The security of this eternal relationship causes a peace regardless of what transpires during our physical life on earth.

Christ's victory changes your life by giving you an eternal outlook on everything that happens to you. The cares and concerns of this life pale in comparison to the eternity we will spend in His presence without these temporal concerns. This eternal perspective gives you the faith needed to believe God for the big future that He has for you. As you understand the depth of His love more and more, you will believe God's plan for your future despite your personal inability to bring it to pass.

Live a life where people marvel and have no other explanation than you have been with God.

This is the abundant life that Jesus came for you to have: a life spent trusting in a loving God who cannot fail you; a life spent dreaming with God about what He can do regardless of your shortcomings. This is a place where people say things about you like, "They did what?" or "How did they do that, they're not that smart?" There will be no other explanation than your relationship with Jesus. Acts 4:13 says it best, *"Now when they saw the boldness of Peter and John, and perceived that they were uneducated and untrained men, they marveled, and realized that they had been with Jesus."* Live a life where people marvel and have no explanation other than you have been with God.

Living life with the knowledge of Christ's victory allows us to enter the place of proving the wisdom of God's plan to all of the eternal beings in the spiritual world. *"To the intent that now the manifold wisdom of God might be made known by the church to the principalities and powers in the heavenly places" (Ephesians 3:10).* Although, in the natural, you might seem to be the most unlikely choice for the fulfillment of God's eternal plans, that very fact shows forth the greatness of our God to all of His creation.

I would like to leave you with this prayer from the apostle Paul for the church. Receive this word of God for yourself because this is what He desires for you:

> *"For this reason I bow my knees to the Father of our Lord Jesus Christ, from whom the whole family in heaven and earth is named, that He would grant You, according to the riches of His glory, to be strengthened with might through His Spirit in the inner man, that Christ may dwell in your hearts through faith; that you, being rooted and grounded in love, may be able to comprehend with all the saints what is the width and length and depth and height- to know the love of Christ which passes knowledge; that you may be filled with all the fullness of God. Now to Him who is able to do exceedingly abundantly above all that we ask or think, according to the power that works in us, to Him be glory in the church by Christ Jesus to all generations, forever and ever" (Ephesians 3:14-21). Amen.*

A Christus Victor, An Historical Study of the Three Main Types of the Idea of Atonement, by Gustaf Aulén © 1931 SPCK, Wipf and Stock Publishers

Extended Outline

Introduction

About The Author

I grew up in church and accepted Jesus as my savior at the age of seven, but did not find myself growing very much spiritually as I got older. Even after re-dedicating my life to God at the age of twenty-one I still did not feel close to God. I was attending church and doing all of the right things. In fact, I was one of the best doers there, but something was missing. There just had to be more to the Christian life.

I started my own service business in 1990 and by 2000 I could do my work and, at the same time, think on something completely different. So, while working I would meditate on bible verses. It was during one of these extended times of thinking on a particular passage of scripture that something began to happen.

For years I would think on 1 Corinthians 2:16 *"For who has known the mind of the Lord that he may instruct Him? But we have the mind of Christ."* I did not see any immediate changes, but I can look back now and see that one specific thought began to permeate my mind: God loved me. I found myself, even on very difficult days of demanding physical labor, being assured that no matter what I was going through; <u>God loved me</u>. I now know I was experiencing the foundational understanding of the mind of Christ. I was receiving the knowledge of God's love.

As this revelation was growing I began to see that other Christians, for the most part, did not have this assurance of God's love. I found myself saying all the time, "It's ok, God loves you." But, I knew I had to do more. Sometime around the summer of 2009 God directed me to attend Charis Bible College in Colorado Springs, Colorado. In the spring of 2013 I founded The Truth Wins Ministries, which is dedicated to overcoming the opposing forces that suppress the knowledge of God's love. This book is the first in a series devoted to that purpose.